WESTERN OUTLAWS

WESTERN

VINCENT PAUL RENNERT

OUTLAWS

★ AMERICA ★
IN THE MAKING

Crowell-Collier Press New York
Collier-Macmillan Limited London

FOR ANNETTA

CONTENTS

INTRODUCTION

DURING THE LATTER HALF OF THE NINETEENTH century the vast, open, majestic West beckoned to people as the land between the Atlantic seaboard and the Mississippi became increasingly populated.

Frontier life was primitive, hard, and sometimes savage and cruel. It attracted courageous, adventurous individuals. Since law and order were slow in coming to an area so far beyond the reach of civilization, the frontier also became a natural haven for drifters and men on the run from the law. Many men had come away from the Civil War embittered, mentally if not physically scarred, and hardened to killing. The James and Younger brothers, for example, cut their teeth in the vicious guerrilla fighting that took place in the Border States, and John Wesley Hardin epitomized the natural result of the postwar residue of hate. While these men were the products of war and racial strife

1

others—like Sam Bass, Butch Cassidy, Billy the Kid, and the Daltons—were the result of social and economic change.

In 1866, the first herds of longhorn cattle had moved north out of Texas to signal the beginning of the cattle industry and the era of the cowboy. By 1867 the movement of cattle to the rich northern markets had reached gigantic proportions. It was a time of prosperity and full employment, and thousands of families left their homes and jobs in the East and headed for the cattle country. The cattle boom continued until 1871, a year when 600,000 longhorns were driven up such famous trails as the Chisholm, Western, and the Shawnee. A faltering market and a vicious winter temporarily slowed the flow of cattle, but by 1873 the trails were again clogged with the great herds.

Signs of impending trouble persisted in the form of a fluctuating market. A depression dropped cattle prices during 1873 and 1874, but by 1876 the economy had stabilized. In 1883 a severe drought decimated the herds; the following year saw a slump in the price of beef; and in 1885, twin disasters dealt the fatal blows—an economic crash and a winter that killed the cattle by the tens of thousands.

The cattle kingdoms collapsed. Unemployment, rustling, and thievery became widespread. Jobless cowboys and ranch hands drifted into the frontier settlements looking for work, excitement or trouble. Thus many outlaws of the American West were as much a natural product of their time as were the gangsters of the 1930's.

*Dime novels of the day painted outlaws like Jesse
James in glowing colors.*

Outlaws like Sam Bass, Billy the Kid, and Jesse James were legends in their own time, their exploits traded over campfires and in bunkhouses, the deeds of robbery and murder often expanded and embroidered to an astonishing degree. In the lonely settlements and the cow towns people took time out from the rigors of their lives to devour the newspaper accounts, or to follow the lurid details set down as "fact" in the "penny dreadfuls" and the dime novels of the day. In time many of these highly fictionalized accounts were accepted as authentic history, serving as the basis for later books and thereby perpetuating the legends.

By such means many outlaws achieved a near-heroic Robin Hood stature, their crimes committed in defense of womanhood, to redress wrongs inflicted upon them by society, or to care for the poor at the expense of the evil rich. Jesse James was painted in such glowing hues—and not only in his own day, as movies and television regularly demonstrate.

Poor Jesse even has had imitators, men who claimed his name and his deeds on the strength of fake documents, a superficial familiarity with the outlaw's personal life and family background, and consummate poise and nerve.

The last pretender died in 1951, maintaining since his appearance in Oklahoma in 1948 that he was the *real* Missouri bandit. Prior to his decision to be Jesse, this gentleman had called himself J. Frank Dalton. His true identity, however, remains unclear. Like others before him this faker held that Jesse had not been assassinated but had instead gone into hiding. This and other claims were easily disproved and Dalton, alias Jesse James, faded away.

The James legends have quite successfully disguised the fact that Jesse, Frank, and the Youngers were brazen, cruel, and desperate killers. With Billy the Kid the situation is the reverse. Billy has gone down in history as a pathological killer, a vicious hoodlum who cut down one man for each of his twenty-one years. The Kid does not deserve that reputation. He killed four men by himself; another half-dozen died at the hands of various groups of which the Kid was a part: no one will ever know whose bullet killed whom.

While some of the outlaws discussed in the following pages were killers, others seemed to go out of their way to cause as little physical harm as possible. Sam Bass was involved in numerous robberies and shot it out with the law on more than one occasion. Yet only in the last days of his life did he participate in a killing, and had it not been for the actions of two bungling deputies who upset a carefully laid trap, the shooting might never have happened. Black Bart managed to become the West's most famous lone stagecoach robber without firing a shot. And the last of the lone train robbers, Bill Carlisle, never hurt a soul.

JOHN
WESLEY
HARDIN

"WES" HARDIN WAS BORN IN BONHAM, TEXAS, ON MAY 26, 1853, and grew into his teens during the Civil War. While still very young he developed a quick temper, a willingness to fight at the drop of a hat, and hatred for Negroes. Among the first Yankee soldiers to return to Texas from the war were many Negroes—former slaves who had joined the Army that set them free. This fueled the fires of bitterness—commingled with an undercurrent of fear—into a firm hatred for anything "Yankee," and when anyone was hurt or when any crime was committed against a Texan, it was assumed that a Yankee must have done it. Conversely, the "Rebs" were automatically at fault should a Yankee or a Negro be killed.

One day in 1868, when Wes was fifteen years old, he rode out to his uncle's ranch to help harvest the cane crop. The boy took along his forty-four caliber pistol. After some work in the field Wes and his cousin, Barnett Jones, stopped to rest and play. They got the idea of challenging Mage, a former slave who worked on the plantation, to a wrestling match. As the three of them rolled around in the dust, Wes scratched Mage's face, drawing blood. Mage, muttering threats, went off to get a gun. When Wes's uncle heard what was going on, he ordered Mage off the ranch. But the following morning, as Wes started his trip home, the two met again. Mage, armed with a stick, grabbed the bridle of the boy's horse. Wes told him to back off. Instead, Mage swung his stick. In return, Wes pulled his pistol and fired three times, but after each hit Mage picked himself up and started at Wes again. In his rage and frustration at being unable to stop Mage, Wes turned and galloped to a nearby house where he told the owner, Judge Holshousen, what had happened. Another neighbor was summoned and the three returned to where Mage now lay bleeding and in pain, but still full of fight. Wes yanked out his pistol again, but Holshousen stopped him. He could see that the man was dying and told Wes to go home and tell his father what had happened.

Mage died from his wounds. Fearful of arrest and trial at the hands of people Wes considered "enemies of the South," he left home to stay near his older brother Joe, who taught school about twenty-five miles north of Sumpter, in Trinity County. His father gave Wes a shotgun in case he needed to protect himself again.

Several days later three soldiers were spotted riding toward the farm where the boy was staying. His brother told him the men were coming, and advised Wes to get moving. Wes rode into the woods, circled around, and ambushed the soldiers as they rode single file across a creek. Two men were felled by his shotgun; the third was brought down by a pistol shot as he tried to flee.

Wes went home. A few days later he and his father set out for Corsicana, Texas, south of Dallas, where Wes got himself a teaching job in a small school. Although his own education was limited he taught about twenty-five pupils between the ages of six and sixteen. Satisfied that his son was now settled and would make good, the father returned home. Wes stayed with the job for three months, doing well enough to be offered the position again for the following year. He turned it down to be a "cowboy," that is, to be free to carry on his private vendetta against the hated Yankees.

By the time Wes turned sixteen, he was spending most of his time learning to drink, gamble, and shoot well. He developed a particular skill with a pistol, mastering the technique of spinning the gun in his hand while never losing control of it, a trick that later proved valuable. He seemed to thrive on being thought of as tough, and he liked to be with men who had reputations for being fighters.

One day, while riding with his nineteen-year-old cousin Simp Dixon near Corsicana, they spotted a small party of soldiers. Simp was a member of the Ku Klux Klan and shared Wes's desire to "kill Yankee soldiers as long as he lived." The boys opened fire, each killing a soldier. Dixon was himself shot and killed by soldiers later during a gunfight in Limestone County. For his part, Wes continued to think of himself as a one-man army, and he defied anyone to stop him in his little war against the bluecoats.

When word of this latest shooting got back to Wes's father he decided to move the family to Navarro County to be nearer to the boy and to try to control him. The family eventually settled in Towash, in Hill County, a town Wes liked because it had a race track.

But if Joe or Mr. Hardin thought they were going to reform Wes they were wrong. While the family was visiting relatives on Christmas day, Wes borrowed his father's horse. He and a racetrack friend, John Collins, ran the horse in a race and won. That night Jim Bradly, a reputed outlaw, invited Wes to sit in on a poker game. Collins tagged along. Wes quickly won all the money—about $600—but claimed that Bradly still owed him $5.00 more. When he demanded the money, Bradly drew a knife. Wes, whose guns and boots had been set in a corner, found them gone. Collins and Wes, barefoot, left the place with Bradly's laughter ringing in their ears. A short time later Wes met Bradly in the street and killed him with two shots from a borrowed pistol. He and Collins raced away.

Mr. Hardin, determined to protect his son, decided to try another tack. He arranged to have Wes work as a farm hand for his uncle, Bob Hardin, near Brenham, Texas. One of Wes's cousins was assigned to ride along with Wes to be sure that he arrived without trouble. They set out late in January of 1870. Some twenty-five miles out of Towash and fifty miles from their destination, they stopped at the town of Horn Hill, where a traveling circus was performing. Hearing that there had been some trouble between the circus people and the town's citizens, they went out to the circus grounds to see what was going on. They joined a group of circus hands around a fire, but before long Wes managed to get into a fight. One of the men punched him in the nose. Wes promptly killed him with one shot.

Wes and his cousin Alec hit the trail, but the next day Alec turned back and Wes continued on alone. He stopped in the town of Kosse, where he visited a prostitute. A young man came bursting in on them, threatening to kill Wes unless he handed over $100. He knew it was a con game routine, so he went through the motions of handing over his money, letting some of it fall to the floor. Wes killed victim number eight when he stooped to pick it up, took the money back, and continued on to the Bob Hardin farm.

He worked there for a while, and his family no doubt relaxed at the prospect of his finally quieting down. What he did in his spare time was another matter. Phil Coe, a notorious gambler operating in Brenham at the time, saw enough of Wes at the gambling tables to give him the nickname of Little Seven-Up, referring to the card game at which he excelled.

It was at this time that Wes learned that he was on the wanted list of the Texas State Police and decided to move on. He chose Evergreen because he had heard that Bill Longley, a well-known outlaw, was in the town and Wes wanted to meet him. He got into a game of seven-up with Ben Hinds, a friend of Longley's, and won $20.00. But when he tried to end the game Hinds became angry and cursed him. Wes pulled his forty-four and Ben apologized. He also promised to introduce Wes to Longley the following day. The two men met, however, in the street that very afternoon. Longley wasted no time in testing Wes. He told the boy that he had heard he was a spy for the state police, and that Wes could get shot if he was not careful. As bystanders watched and waited, the two men stood face to face. Finally, Wes answered Longley's charge: "You believe a damned lie. All I ask is a fair fight, and if your name is Bill Longley I want you to understand that you can't bulldoze or scare me."

Longley grinned, good-naturedly slapped Wes on the

Wes pulled his forty-four and Ben apologized.

back, and invited him to play some poker. Wes went along, beat Longley in the game, and rode off disappointed in his hero.

Wes Hardin was now seventeen. He returned to his family, who were now living in Mount Calm, only to find that a reward of $800 was offered by the state police for his arrest. Of 2,870 men wanted by the police, Wes's name led the list. He promptly packed up and set off for Round Rock, near Austin. He then moved on to Marshall, Texas, where, being mistaken for someone else, he was arrested for a shooting for which he was not responsible. While in jail awaiting transfer to Waco, he bought a smuggled-in pistol and tied it under his arm beneath his shirt. It was January and bitter cold when the time came for his transfer. He had to ride without a saddle. His feet were tied together under the belly of his horse, and his hands were firmly bound. It was to be a two-hundred-mile trip. He knew that when he got to Waco he would be recognized.

On the second night out Wes's hands were untied when the party stopped to camp. While one of the two guards went to a farmhouse to get feed for the horses, Wes pulled his hidden gun and killed the remaining guard.

He rode to Mount Calm, told his father what had happened, and rode off again several days later. After three nights out he came back. He had killed three more state policemen, who had captured him while he was asleep. His captors had set off with him for Austin. On the way he caught one guard unaware and killed him, then shot the other two when they awakened and reached for their guns. On January 12, 1871, Wes, accompanied by his father for about seventy miles, headed for Mexico. After his father had turned back, Wes decided instead to visit some relatives in Gonzales County. They were putting up herds for a trail drive. Wes agreed to help out.

During the cattle drive Wes added two Indians to his list of victims: one was killed while Wes was chasing a wild turkey in the brush. The second one was part of an Indian party that intercepted the herd and demanded one of the steers.

Farther on in the drive Wes was annoyed by another herd coming up from behind. He warned the Mexican trail boss to stay back, but instead the man went to get his pistol. He returned, fired, and missed. Wes pulled the trigger of his own gun, but it failed to fire; the same thing happened with the Mexican's next try. Both men then got off their horses and began a fistfight. It was a draw. Both sides withdrew to get ready for more serious action. When the Mexicans returned, six-strong, Wes and Jim Clements, a cousin, charged them head-on. When the shooting stopped, all six Mexicans lay dead, Wes having accounted for five of them.

Abilene was the end of the trail. Here, on April 5, Wild Bill Hickok had begun his short term as marshal. Hardin, now eighteen, rode into the town on the first of June, 1871.

Hardin did not remain in Abilene for very long. One night he and another man were eating dinner when three men came in. They had been drinking heavily and soon started loudly cursing Texas and Texans. Wes

went over to them and announced that he was from
Texas. Guns roared on both sides; another man fell
dying.

Wes headed for the Carol-Johnson camp on the
North Cottonwood River. Here, he learned that Bill
Cohron, a friend of his, had been killed by a Mexican
known only as Bideno. The cowmen asked Wes to
take on the job of hunting the man down. On June
27 he and a fellow by the name of Jim Rodgers headed
across Kansas on Bideno's trail.

Near Newton, Kansas, they were joined by Cohron's
brother John and a trail driver named Hugh Anderson.
They caught up with Bideno later the following day,
while he was having a meal in the town of Bluff Creek.
Wes killed Bideno as he reached for a gun.

*Hardin rode into
Abilene, Kansas,
the end of the trail.*

After leaving the townspeople $20.00 to cover the cost of burial, Wes and his friends started back. On the way word reached them that Hickok was telling people that if Hardin returned to Abilene he would kill him. They met in town, however, and there was no trouble. Wes was allowed to keep his guns on so long as his friends removed their weapons.

Early that July, Manning and Gip Clements rode into Abilene. Manning told Wes that he had killed two men in his trail outfit who had attacked him. Wes promised to have things "squared" with Hickok so that he would not be arrested. But the man who was to take care of this for Wes, Columbus Carol, got drunk and it slipped his mind. Wes, meanwhile, had asked Manning and Gip to turn in their guns. That evening Hickok

15

found the three men eating and put Manning under arrest. Wes took Hickok aside and asked that Manning be freed as a favor. Hickock agreed that while Manning would go along to jail, he would be freed at midnight. That evening, Hickok and Hardin took in the town together. Wild Bill slipped the jail key to Wes around eleven-thirty. Wes passed it to a friend who then let Manning out.

After seeing Manning safely away, Wes and Gip remained in town. The following night, as Wes was sleeping, a man crept into his room with a knife. Wes woke up, pulled his gun from under the pillow and emptied it into the man. Nevertheless, the man got away, taking Wes's pants with him. Wes was now unarmed, having given his other pistol to Manning. Gip had left his pistols at camp. Wes looked out the front window and saw Hickok and his men entering the hotel. Wes and Gip climbed out of the window and made their separate ways out of town.

Wes hid in a haystack until a cowboy appeared. The man lost his horse at the point of Wes's empty pistol. As Wes mounted, he was spotted by three posse-men. He dashed off with the riders in pursuit. Wes outdistanced them to the Columbus Carol camp, put on a pair of pants and armed himself. When the three men rode up, Wes got the drop on them, took their guns, boots, and pants, and sent them back to Abilene lighter but probably wiser.

Gip and Wes rendezvoused in Cottonwood, then went on to Texas where they found Manning. The three of them went to Manning's home in Gonzales County in August 1871.

Not long afterward, while Wes was in a grocery store, two state policemen rode up. Obviously aware of Hardin's presence, one of the men waited outside while his partner entered the store, gun drawn. He ordered Wes to hand over his guns. The outlaw started to comply, holding out his guns butt first. But as the policeman reached to take them Hardin spun one around in his hand and fired, killing the officer with a bullet in the head. The second lawman started shooting into the store, but he was wounded by Wes's return fire and rode off. A month later a posse came down from Austin to get Wes, but he had been tipped off. He was ready for them, killing three before they quit the fight.

Early in 1872 Wes married Jane Bowen. Two months later he decided to gather and trail drive a bunch of horses east to Louisiana for resale, planning to start his return trip in July. Typically, Hardin found himself in no end of trouble during the trip. At one point he left his herd of horses in the care of others and rode ahead to Hemphill, Texas, for some gambling. While there a state policeman arrested a man for carrying a pistol. Wes thought the charge unfair and pleaded the man's case. This resulted in a new trial and a subsequent acquittal. Later, outside the courthouse, a boy started needling the policeman who had arrested the man. According to Hardin, the policeman threatened the boy. Wes stepped in, and as the policeman started to draw his pistol Wes pulled both a derringer and a six-shooter. He fired with the smaller gun, hitting the policeman in the shoulder. The outlaw fled a sheriff's posse and rejoined his herd, selling them on July 27 and heading back home.

17

On August 7 he rode into Trinity City, Texas, and was soon busy gambling in a bowling alley. An argument over the stakes arose with a man named Sublet who, angered, stalked out and got himself a shotgun. Sublet came back and stood out in the street. When Wes appeared in the bowling alley's doorway the man fired but missed his target. Wes was about to return the fire when a drunk, armed with a knife, grabbed him, claiming that together they could whip anybody. Wes struggled to get loose, but as he did he found himself by the door, giving Sublet another shot. This time the shotgun found its mark. Wes, bleeding profusely, chased Sublet through a store, hitting the fleeing man once before he got away.

Wes was not expected to live. A week later, however, he was told that if he did not leave he would be arrested. He was taken to Sulphur Spring, then to Sumpter, and then into Angelina County to the home of Dave Harrel, an old friend. But the law kept after him, and at the beginning of September two men approached the Harrel house armed with rifles. Hardin dropped both men with his shotgun, but not before being hit in the thigh himself. Now wounded again, and still bothered by his earlier wounds, he knew he had little chance to escape another posse. He asked Harrel to go and tell the sheriff he was ready to surrender. When the lawmen arrived, Wes was asked to give up his guns. As he reached for one, a member of the posse thought he was making a false move and Wes was shot in the right knee.

Hardin was eventually brought to Gonzales and

placed in jail. Early that October he sawed the bars of his cell and escaped, returning home to his wife. Here he rested until January, 1873, when he began driving and shipping cattle. In April he went to Cuero, a shipping point, to take care of some business. While there he dropped by a bar and joined a poker game. After winning the pot, Wes went to the bar for a drink. A man named Morgan figured the flush Hardin ought to buy him a bottle of champagne and when the outlaw refused, Morgan pulled a gun. Wes did too, killing the man with one shot.

Hardin was already the most wanted outlaw in the West when, on May 17, he shotgunned Sheriff Jack

When the outlaw refused to buy him a bottle of champagne, Morgan pulled a gun. Wes killed him with one shot.

Helms, who was attempting to arrest Jim Taylor, a friend of Wes's, for shooting a man in a pool-hall fight. After Hardin downed the sheriff, Taylor finished him off with a pistol. The next day some fifty men rode out to get Wes, but he was alerted. That night he gathered fourteen men and rode to where he knew the posse was bedded down. His plan was to shoot the men as they slept, but before he could get his chance another posse arrived. Meanwhile, the outlaws' ranks had been swelled enough to even the fight. A truce was called and all hands went their own ways.

Hardin, along with Taylor, went back to work driving cattle. Stopping in Comanche, Wes heard that Charles Webb, the deputy sheriff from Brown County, with a posse of fifteen men, was looking for him. Webb and Hardin met in town and, when the outlaw turned his back, the sheriff pulled a gun. Wes turned, both men firing at once. Webb fell dead; Wes was hit in the side. A menacing crowd gathered quickly, shouting for a hanging. The outlaw left town in a hurry.

He was now in serious trouble. Large parties of men were systematically hunting the countryside for him. On June 1, Hardin, Taylor, Alec Barrickman, and Ham Anderson were camped in a valley several miles outside Comanche when they were discovered by a band of more than one hundred riders. Under the cover of darkness the party quietly led away the horses belonging to Barrickman and Anderson. Discovering the loss, Wes and Taylor rode off to get more horses. The other two men headed on foot for a prearranged meeting place. There they all mounted and split in two's—

Hardin and Taylor riding together. But they did not get far. Armed men were everywhere. The two outlaws put their horses at full gallop. Pursued by a posse, they reached the top of a hill to find themselves cut off by about two hundred riders. Wes and Taylor started down the hill, with the other posse coming down in back of them. Suddenly, the outlaws turned their horses and dashed right back up the hill at the pursuing posse. In the confusion they got away and headed for a friend's ranch outside of Austin, reaching there on June 5.

There, Hardin learned that a mob had hanged his brother, along with his cousins Tom and Bud Dixon, and that Anderson and Barrickman had been tracked down and shot to death. Wes moved on, with the posses never far behind. He finally fled to New Orleans where he joined his wife and child. They then moved to Gainesville, Florida.

Wes seemed safe at last. He went into business as a saloon owner. Peace and quiet lasted about a week. Wes and some friends decided to pass sentence on a Negro who had been jailed on a rape charge. They set fire to the jail that night, burning the man to death. The Gainesville coroner, however, took care of any problem that might have come up by claiming that the prisoner had set the jail on fire himself. The coroner had been with Hardin that night.

Wes then moved to Micanopy, Florida, where he bought another bar. He subsequently sold out in May 1875 to devote his time to the cattle business. Pinkerton detectives succeeded in tracing him, but he was tipped off and got away. Detectives overtook Wes and another man at the Florida-Georgia line. When the fight ended, two of the lawmen lay dead. Wes then made his way to Polland, Alabama, where his wife and two children, Molly and John, had gone. He went into the logging business, apparently doing quite well.

On July 23, 1877, Hardin and his business partner, Shep Hardie, went to Pensacola, Florida, to buy supplies. The work finished, they boarded the train for Polland. The Texas Rangers, having received a tip on Hardin's whereabouts, surrounded the station and placed men in the train. After a fierce struggle in the smoking car, where he had been puffing on his meerschaum pipe and playing poker, Wes was finally overpowered.

Taken back to Comanche, Wes was tried and convicted for the murder of Charles Webb. In September, 1878, he received a twenty-five-year sentence at hard labor. He entered the prison at Huntsville, Alabama, on October 5.

After repeated attempts to escape, Wes resigned himself to prison. He started to study theology in 1880 and was soon appointed superintendent of the prison's Sunday school. He also continued his law studies.

On February 17, 1894, he was pardoned and released from prison. His wife had died during his stay in prison, but he returned to Gonzales to be with his children. While there he began a law practice, remarried, and in 1895 moved to El Paso.

It was in El Paso, on August 19, 1895, that a policeman by the name of John Selman arrested Mrs. McRose, Wes's mistress, for carrying a gun. That evening Wes met the elder John Selman, a constable, telling him that his son was a coward for making the arrest when he, Wes, was not present. The elder Selman was not one to let an insult go by unattended.

Later that same evening Hardin was standing at the bar of the Acme saloon, shooting dice with the bartender. Selman drew his gun and shot John Wesley Hardin in the back of his head, killing him.

THE JAMES-YOUNGER GANG

JESSE WOODSON JAMES WAS BORN TO ROBERT AND
Zerelda James on September 5, 1847, near Centerville
(now Kearney) in Clay County, Missouri. His brother
Frank had been born nearly five years earlier on January 10, 1843.

Their parents were Kentuckians. The father, a Bap-
tist preacher, left the family after ten years of marriage
and went to California's gold fields to make his fortune.
He died about three weeks after reaching his destination, at the age of twenty-six.

Mrs. James remarried in 1851, but it was not a good
match and she soon divorced her fifty-year-old second
husband. She married again in 1857. Her third husband, Reuben Samuel, was a doctor and a farmer.
They made their home near Lee's Summit, where the
Younger family lived.

The James brothers grew into their teens at the time

24

of the wild and vicious border war between the anti-slavery Kansas "Jayhawkers" or "Red Legs," and the pro-slavery Missouri "Bushwhackers." The two sides formed guerrilla bands that operated throughout the Civil War.

Following the bombardment of Fort Sumter in April 1861, Frank James enlisted in the Missouri State Guard of the Confederate Army. Shortly after the rout of Federal troops at Bull Run in July, he went into action near Springfield, Missouri. Home on furlough later, he was jailed by Federal militia for his Confederate sentiments and freed several days later when he signed an oath of loyalty to the Union.

Frank promptly joined Quantrill's guerillas, as did Thomas Coleman ("Cole") and Jim Younger, and took part in the ruthless sacking of Lawrence, Kansas, on August 20, 1863.

The same year Jesse James, at the age of sixteen, joined up with "Bloody Bill" Anderson's band. Like Quantrill, Anderson was a wild man who showed no mercy to the victims of his raids. Jesse developed well under Anderson's leadership, becoming an expert rider and gunman. He took part in many raids, leading one near Independence, Missouri, in which twelve Federal soldiers, trapped in a brothel, were shot down.

In the fall of 1863 Jesse led three other men against a picket post near Wellington, killing the eight men there. Over sixty men were killed a few weeks later when thirty guerrillas, headed by George Todd and Jesse, attacked an infantry wagon train. Jesse killed

The James and Younger boys took part in the ruthless sacking of Lawrence, Kansas, in 1863.

nine more Union soldiers at Centralia; nine others in a battle with troops sent in pursuit, two more in the Cherokee Nation—one a chaplain; and, in a pitched battle with Federal Cherokees, fifty-two men out of seventy-five were killed by Jesse's band of twenty-six.

The raiders returned to Missouri from Texas in March of 1865. Crossing the border they were attacked by a Federal patrol. When the battle finally broke off, Jesse could count another man dead.

Finally, weary of being hounded by the Federals, Jesse decided to surrender, and on April 1 he and six of his men rode for Lexington. During the afternoon his group was met by cavalry and attacked. Jesse killed one man but was severely wounded himself with a bullet through his right lung, and his men scattered. Jesse escaped and was found by a Southern sympathizer who took him in. It was at first thought that he would die of his wound, but in the fall of 1865 he was brought back home to Clay County by wagon, weak but still alive.

Jesse was still home recovering from his wound when, on February 13, 1866, the first bank robbery in America took place. The site was the Clay County Savings and Loan Bank at Liberty, Missouri.

There were ten men in the gang: four dismounted and entered, while the rest stayed on their horses. Inside, the cashier, Greenup Bird, and his son were getting set for another day's work. It was eight o'clock when they looked up to face the outlaw's six-shooters. The two frightened employees were herded into the vault as the gang filled a wheat sack with $15,000 in gold. Before they left the outlaws slammed the vault door shut on the two bank clerks. The men then mounted, swung around, fired their guns into the air and raced away. At that moment, George Wynmore, a nineteen-year-old, was leaving his house for a class at William Jewell College. The ten riders galloped by. The young man turned and started to run for home. One of the outlaws wheeled about and fired four times, killing Wynmore.

America's second bank robbery came in October, when a small band held up Alexander & Company at

Lexington; the third, involving five armed riders, occurred on March 2, 1867, in Savannah, Missouri; and the fourth on May 23 at Richmond, Missouri, where fourteen men got $4,000 in gold. At some point, probably Lexington, the James brothers joined the gang.

The Richmond robbery left three dead as the gang fought a shooting duel with aroused citizens after the holdup. Later three of the gang were tracked down and lynched—one near Richmond; the two others outside Warrensburg, in Johnson County. Both Jesse and Frank had a prearranged alibi for the day of the robbery.

The gang did not go into action again until May 20, 1868, when they struck the Russellville, Kentucky, bank for approximately $14,000. Then on December 7, 1869, Jesse, Frank, and Cole Younger held up the bank in Gallatin, Missouri. Jesse murdered the cashier when he balked at opening the safe. The three dashed out of town ahead of a quickly formed posse and escaped.

The gang withdrew to the safety of Clay County, where friendships were strong and Jesse could count on loyal local support. The gang remained quiet until mid-1871 when, on June 3, they turned up in Corydon, Iowa, to snatch $40,000 from the Obocock Brothers Bank. The gang at this time was made up of Jesse and Frank, Jim Cummins, Charlie Pitts, Ed Miller, and the three Youngers—Cole, Jim, and John.

It was nearly a year later when they struck again. On April 12, 1872, they hit the Deposit Bank in Columbia, Kentucky. It was a brutal and unrewarding robbery. Jesse demanded that the cashier give him the keys to the safe, and, when the man refused, Jesse fired three times at point-blank range, killing him. He then blazed away at the safe, but the door held. The outlaws grabbed what they could from the cash drawer and fled with $200.

Sainte Genevieve, Missouri, was next, netting them $4,000. Then, on September 23, a three-man gang grabbed $8,000 in gate receipts at the Kansas City Fair. Whether this was Jesse's work has not been proved.

On July 21 the gang—Jesse and Frank, Cole and Jim Younger, Clell Miller, Bob Moore, and a half-breed called Comanche Tony—held up their first train near Adair, Iowa. They loosened some railroad ties to stop the train. It worked. The resulting crash derailed seven cars. The boiler burst, scalding the engineer to death and severely burning the fireman. The $7,000 loot from the robbery was much less than the gang had hoped for. Actually, they had robbed the wrong train: the one they wanted, loaded with $75,000, passed through Adair twelve hours later.

The gang struck next on January 15, 1874, in Arkansas. They robbed a stagecoach this time, getting over $2,000 from the express package and the fourteen passengers. On January 31 five of the outlaws were back in Missouri to rob the Little Rock Express at Gadshill. They rode into the town and surrounded the train depot, making prisoners of the station agent and several others who had come down to watch the express roar through. Clell Miller planted the trainman's flag in the tracks to halt the train. After robbing the passengers—they got $5,000 from one—they entered the baggage car and gathered up another $2,000.

The gang then split up, the James boys and the Youngers traveling together to Monegaw Springs, Missouri, where the Youngers had a hideout. Jesse and Frank then rode on to Independence, where Jesse married Zerelda Mimms on April 24. Zerelda—whose first name was the same as Jesse's mother's—was his first cousin and had been his girlfriend for nine years. Frank eloped that same year with Annie Ralston, a girl of seventeen.

Meanwhile, the Pinkerton National Detective Agency (founded in 1850, it pioneered in crime fighting) determined to bring down the gang, assigning some of its best men to the job. But it was not to be. Two Pinkerton men and a former deputy, posing as horse and cattle buyers, got on the trail of the Youngers. They stopped at Ted Snuffer's farmhouse to ask directions. Jim and John Younger happened to be there but the lawmen did not see them. The Youngers were suspicious of the strangers and followed them when they left the farm. John, armed with a shotgun, and Jim, carrying two pistols, caught up with the trio about a mile from the Snuffer place and ordered them to halt. One of the Pinkerton men spurred his horse and got away; the other was mortally wounded by John's shotgun— but not before he pulled a concealed pistol and got off a shot that killed John. Jim Younger shot and killed the ex-deputy.

Jesse and his bride were staying with the Samuels, Jesse's mother and stepfather, when another Pinkerton man, disguised as a farmhand looking for work, reached the Samuels' place. Tipped off, Jesse grabbed the detective and took him away; the following day he was found dead. But the Pinkertons pressed the hunt, sending one more "farmhand" into the outlaws' territory. He succeeded in landing a job on a farm near the Samuels'. On January 5, 1875, word reached Pinkerton headquarters that Jesse and Frank were at the Samuels' place. The signal was given to strike, and a posse surrounded the house. Someone tossed a flare lamp inside to illuminate the interior, but Dr. Samuel kicked it into the fireplace. It exploded, killing Jesse's eight-year-old half-brother, Archie, severing Mrs. Samuel's right arm, and wounding the doctor and a servant. Jesse and Frank were not there. The incident sharpened the Samuels' belief that their sons were being persecuted for their guerrilla activities, and increased their determination to shield them whenever possible.

In April the farmer who had unwittingly employed the Pinkerton undercover man was shot in the back by three riders. They were believed to be Jesse, Frank, and Clell Miller, but this was never proved.

The gang got back to business on December 12, 1875, robbing a train at Muncie, Indiana, of about $60,000 in gold, jewels, and cash. This holdup was followed by a stagecoach robbery outside of Austin, Texas, on May 12, 1876, from which the gang realized about $3,000. Next, in July, came the robbery of a Missouri-Pacific train near Otterville, Missouri, the last strike before Northfield, Minnesota—one of the most famous "shoot-outs" in outlaw history.

The robbery took place on September 7. The target was the First National Bank of Northfield. In the gang were the two Jameses, the three Youngers, Bill Chad-well, Clell Miller, and Charlie Pitts.

The gang started out from Fort Osage Township, Missouri, in August, scouting possible hold-up sites as they headed toward Northfield. In fact, on Saturday, September 2, they looked over a bank in Mankato, Minnesota, and moved in to rob it on Monday. But as the gang rode toward the bank they saw a crowd of men turn to look at them. The gang kept on riding, convinced of a trap. Actually, the group of citizens was harmless; they had turned to gaze at the outlaws only because someone had remarked about the magnificent horse Jesse was riding.

On Thursday, just after two o'clock, Jesse, Pitts, and Bob Younger rode into Northfield, dismounting in front of the bank. They strolled up the street and sat for a while in front of a store until Clell Miller and Cole Younger appeared, walking their horses. Jesse, Pitts, and Bob Younger then went into the bank. Cole stopped in the middle of the street and pretended to work on his saddle while keeping an eye out for trouble. Clell hitched his horse and stood outside the door of the bank.

The town was quiet and peaceful. Too much so, for almost any activity was bound to draw attention.

Two men were sitting idly in the sun—one a vacationing University of Michigan student, the other the owner of a hardware store. J. A. Allen, the hardware merchant, noticed the movements of the men. He felt something was wrong, and started for the bank. But as he got near the door Clell grabbed him and pulled a gun. Allen, however, broke clear and dashed away

The James-Younger gang. Standing: Cole and Bob Younger; seated: Frank and Jesse James.

shouting the alarm. The student picked up the cry. Clell fired at him but missed as the young man scrambled to safety. Cole and Miller remounted as Chadwell, Jim Younger, and Frank James galloped in, guns blazing, to drive the alerted citizens to cover.

Three employees were inside the bank when Jesse, Pitts, and Bob entered: J. L. Heywood, the bookkeeper-cashier; F. J. Wilcox, the assistant bookkeeper; and A. E. Bunker, the teller. Jesse demanded that the safe be opened. Heywood replied that the safe was time-locked. Pitts lost his temper and smashed Heywood over the head with his gun butt. The outlaw then pulled a knife and slashed at Heywood's throat wounding him slightly. Pitts and Younger jammed their guns into the dazed man's stomach, telling him to open the vault. He still refused. Pitts held his gun near the cashier's head and pulled the trigger, but the bullet only grazed him. Jesse and Bob turned their attention to the other two men, knocking them down in an effort to get them to open the vault, but without success. A search was begun for the cash box. Bunker, finding his chance, broke for the rear door. Pitts fired, but missed as the man tumbled down the back steps and headed up the alley. Pitts got to the door and fired again, this time hitting the teller in the shoulder.

The outlaws knew they had better make their break. Pitts dashed out, but as Bob and Jesse headed for the door, Heywood started to struggle to his feet. One of the outlaws turned and shot him through the head.

When the three men emerged into the sunlight they ran head-on into heavy fire from guns aimed from the windows and doorways facing the bank. One terrified citizen tried to run across the street and was gunned down by a mounted outlaw. In return, Miller was hit in the face by a shotgun blast, but he stayed in the saddle and continued to fire. Cole Younger was hit next, receiving a minor wound. Chadwell was the first of the gang killed, a bullet through the heart fired from a distance of seventy-five yards. Miller was then hit again. He tumbled from his horse and died a few moments later. A bullet smashed into Bob Younger's right elbow; he shifted his gun to his left hand and continued shooting.

The fight was hopeless. The remaining outlaws dashed out of the Northfield inferno and headed for safety. But there was no easy escape. Dogged by hundreds of mounted posse-men, the gang was forced to split, the following Tuesday, September 12, having abandoned their horses Sunday. Jesse and Frank stayed together and managed to escape on stolen mounts.

The three Youngers and Charlie Pitts tried to make their way out of the posse-infested area on foot. Two weeks later they were trapped near Madelia, and a posse closed in. When the firing stopped, Pitts was dead, shot five times. Bob Younger was hit twice; Jim five times; Cole eleven.

The three survivors stood trial on November 9, receiving life sentences to the state prison at Stillwater, Minnesota.

After their escape from Northfield Jesse and Frank fled to Clay County, where they picked up their wives and went on to Nashville, Tennessee. Jesse later moved to Kansas City for a while, next to California, and finally back to Clay County where he formed a new band of outlaws.

The gang included Jesse and Frank, Tucker Basham, Wood Hite, Dick Liddell, Ed Miller (Clell's brother), and Bill Ryan. Their first target was Blue Cut, near Glendale, Missouri. Here, they held up the Chicago & Alton Railroad train on October 7, 1879, escaping with $35,000 after pistol-whipping the express messenger.

They struck next at Muscle Shoals, Alabama, some seventeen months later, robbing a stage; on July 10 they showed up in Riverton, Iowa, getting $5,000 from the Davis & Sexton Bank. And a week later, on July 15, they robbed the Chicago, Rock Island & Pacific Railroad's No. 2, bound from Kansas City to Davenport, Iowa.

Three of the gang, including Jesse, boarded the train when it stopped at Cameron, taking seats in the smoking car. Two more swung aboard that evening as it was pulling out of Winston, making their way forward on the roof of the baggage car. Suddenly, the three outlaws in the smoker pulled their guns, fired, and ordered everyone to raise his hands. Then, without warning, one of the outlaws let loose at the conductor who was standing a short distance away in the aisle. Again and again the outlaw fired, driving the conductor back down the aisle until he collapsed on the platform between cars and tumbled off the train dead.

The passengers scrambled for the exit at the other end of the car, but one of them, Frank McMillan, tried to re-enter. He was shot and killed by Frank James. Meanwhile, the two other bandits reached the cab and forced the engineer to halt the train. The men then went to the express car, beating the messenger until he gave in and opened the safe. It contained only $600.

The law was now everywhere, Jesse and the gang were "hot" and the rewards for their capture mounted. Yet, on September 7, 1881, the gang struck again at Blue Cut. Once more they got only a small amount: $600 from the express car and about $1,500 from the passengers. This time the gang consisted of Wood and Clarence Hite, Dick Liddell, Charlie Ford and Frank and Jesse.

The end of the road was near. The gang fell apart for good. Jesse and Ed Miller, who had been in on the first Blue Cut strike, headed for Missouri together, but only Jesse made it. For reasons never made clear, Jesse had murdered Miller. Liddell killed Wood Hite in a scrap over the division of the Blue Cut spoils. Liddell later gave himself up and implicated the gang in the various robberies—not sparing Wood's brother Clarence, who was arrested and sentenced to twenty-five years in prison.

It was the end of the road for Jesse, too. On April 3, 1882, Jesse, and Charlie and Bob Ford, were together in St. Joseph to plan a bank robbery. Unknown to Jesse, Bob Ford had made plans to kill him for the reward money—some $10,000. Bob let his brother in on the scheme and together they met Jesse and agreed to join up with him.

Just after eight o'clock on that Monday morning, the three men entered Jesse's house. Here is Charlie Ford's account of what happened:

> *Well, we had come in from the barn where we had been feeding and currying the horses, and Jesse complained of being warm and pulled off his coat and threw it on the bed and opened the door, and said that he guessed he would pull off the [gun] belt as some person might see it.*
>
> *Then he went to brush off some pictures, and when he turned his back I gave my brother the*

wink and we both pulled our pistols, but he, my brother, was the quickest and fired first. I had my finger on the trigger and was just going to fire, but I saw his shot was a death shot and did not fire. He heard us cock our pistols and turned his head. The ball struck him in the back of the head and he fell.

Jesse James was dead at the age of thirty-four. Frank James gave himself up on October 5, 1882, a tired and beaten man of thirty-eight who was sick of running. Asked why he had surrendered, Frank said,

I was tired of an outlaw's life. I have been hunted for twenty-one years. I have literally lived in the saddle. I have never known a day of perfect peace. It was one long, anxious, inexorable, eternal virgil. When I slept it was literally in the midst of an arsenal. If I heard dogs bark more fiercely than usual, or the feet of horses in a greater volume of sound than usual, I stood to my arms. Have you any idea of what a man must endure who leads such a life? No, you cannot. No one can unless he lives it for himself.

Frank James was tried and acquitted of the McMillan murder, and an indictment against him for the Blue Cut robbery was dismissed. A year later he was tried for still another robbery, but again there was insufficient direct evidence and he was acquitted. As a result, Frank never had to serve a prison sentence for his crimes. He died on February 18, 1915.

As for the Youngers, Bob died of tuberculosis on

September 16, 1889, while still in prison. He was thirty-two years old. Jim and Cole were paroled on July 11, 1901, after serving almost twenty-five years. A year later Jim committed suicide in St. Paul, Minnesota. Cole lived to be seventy-two, dying on March 21, 1916, at Lee's Summit, Missouri.

Jesse James was dead at thirty-four.

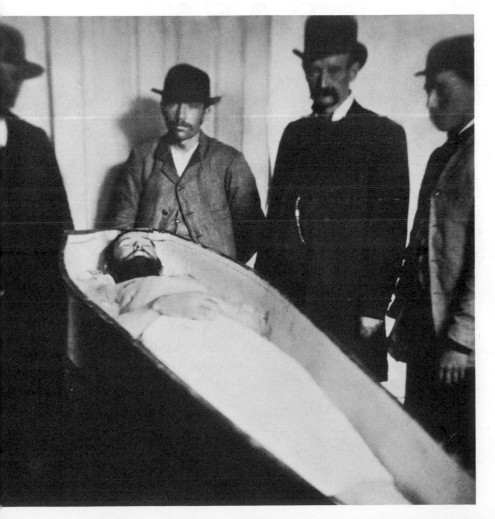

SAM
BASS

SAM BASS WAS BORN ON A FARM NEAR MITCHELL,
Indiana, on July 21, 1851, to Daniel and Elizabeth
Bass. He was one of ten children, two of whom died
in infancy. Another brother was killed fighting as a
member of the Sixteenth Indiana Regiment, during
the Civil War.

Bass's mother died on June 3, 1861, at the age of
thirty-nine. Sam was ten years old. His father then
married a woman with two children by a previous marriage. She gave birth to Sam's stepbrother shortly before Daniel Bass died of pneumonia at the age of forty-
two on February 20, 1864.

Sam's Uncle Solomon was appointed administrator
of the Bass estate. He rented out the 175-acre Bass
farm and sold the father's effects. Sam, now thirteen
years old, went to live with another uncle, David
Sheeks, who had a place about two miles from the old

homestead. In 1869 Sam left the farm, traveling to St. Louis for a short stay, then on to Rosedale, Mississippi, where he remained for a year working in a sawmill. When he was nineteen years old, Sam headed for Texas to satisfy his yen to be a cowboy.

He worked during the spring and winter of 1871 on a ranch by Denton Creek, some fourteen miles southwest of Denton. Preferring the bustle of town life, however, he moved into Denton, where he got work as a stable hand at a hotel. This job lasted for about eighteen months, and Sam then signed on as a ranch hand and teamster for W. F. Egan, who had a twelve-acre place in Denton. Here, Sam made friends with Frank Jackson, Henry Underwood, and Jim Murphy, men who would play important roles later in his career.

Denton changed Sam. He hung around with a tough crowd, and developed a liking for whiskey and gambling. He was not an imposing figure, hardly fitting the picture some people had of how a tough outlaw should look. He stood five feet eight inches tall, weighed in at about 140 pounds, and often went for a week or so without shaving. He dressed carelessly and walked with a slight stoop.

There was a horse track just outside Denton, and Sam could be found there every Sunday afternoon. He took a partner, Armstrong Egan, W. F. Egan's brother, and together they bought a horse that they named Jenny. The partnership did not last long. Armstrong's brother demanded that he quit horse racing and sell out his share to Sam. Finally, Sam's race track activities so annoyed his boss that he was given the choice

Sam Bass was not a menacing figure, hardly the stereotype of an outlaw.

of selling the horse or quitting his job. Sam's love for the horse won out. He quit his job and gave his full time to horse racing.

Jenny's fame and success spread. The horse became known as the Denton Mare and was raced against all comers, winning all but one race. Sam's character, meanwhile, began to change. He grew increasingly reckless and wild. He played the horses, gambled at cards, drank heavily, and sought the company of the town's rougher men.

Horse racing got Sam into his first scrape in the late fall of 1874. Constable Marcus Millner's horse won a race against Sam's mare, but Sam claimed a foul. Ultimately the case went to civil court. Sam won by default when Millner failed to appear. His growing reputation for irresponsibility was not helped when he then proceeded to ignore a promissory note he had given his lawyers.

Sam's next brush with the law came when he and some friends got into a brawl at a dance, which resulted in the knifing of the fiddler. Although Sam was credited with saving the life of a deputy sheriff who tried to break up the fight, he and the others were arrested for the stabbing. The case was dismissed.

A short time later Sam, Henry Underwood, and some other friends took the Denton Mare into Indian Territory to race against horses owned by the Choctaws and the Cherokees. Despite the Denton Mare's victories, the Indians refused to give up the horses they had wagered. Sam challenged them to another race, but told his rider to keep on going to a prearranged meeting place after crossing the finish line. Sam's horse won, the Indians balked at paying up, and that night Sam and the others helped themselves to some of the Indians' horses—many more than had been wagered—and fled to San Antonio, where the horses were sold.

Late in 1875 Sam and the others returned to Denton, making their camp on nearby Hickory Creek. One night while he and Underwood were leaving Denton with supplies, Sam dropped a watermelon to the street. Some bystanders laughed about the accident and ridiculed the riders. Sam and Henry were not amused. They jumped from their horses and began to throw stones at the group. Everyone scattered, but Underwood managed to grab one of the men and was about to beat him with a club when a deputy sheriff appeared and tried to take Henry in. He and Sam broke free and galloped out of town, eluding the posse sent after them.

Bass, Underwood, and John Hudson—Sam's rider in the Indian Territory races—split and headed for the safety of southwestern Texas, Underwood to try his hand at trailing cattle. Hudson was not heard from again. Sam went to San Antonio, where he met Joel Collins, a sometime cowboy who had been tried and acquitted in 1870 for the murder of a man named Bedal Rosalees. Collins owned a bar in San Antonio, but he sold out shortly after taking up with Sam. The two men worked out a horse race deal to cheat unsuspecting challengers. The scheme called for Collins to act as the Denton Mare's owner, while Sam pretended to be a horse trainer. Sam would get work with a man who had a race horse. He would check the horse over, test it for speed, and if he thought the Denton Mare could beat it he would urge the owner to race against Collins. Sam also suggested that the owner and his friends bet heavily on the outcome of the race. The Denton Mare always won, much to the profit of Bass and Collins. It was easy work, but they soon tired of the game. Joel suggested that they gather a herd of cattle for a drive north, where the steers were in demand.

In the summer of 1876 they started up the trail to Dodge City with about 700 cattle, stopping off in that wild town to take on supplies and have some fun before moving the herd farther north where prices were better.

They sold the cattle for a handsome profit, even after paying off their riders. Sam and Joel then rode on to Ogallala. They saw the sights, which were considerable even by Dodge City standards, before riding off to the Black Hills in Dakota Territory. They landed in Deadwood, a den of thieves, gamblers, and easy women. For the first time Bass was outsmarted: he lost at gambling and bought a quartz mine that turned out to be worthless.

Almost as a last resort the two men tried freighting between Deadwood and Cheyenne. Sam made the first trip—and went $60 in the hole. Jack Davis, a new friend of Sam's, took the four-horse freighting team on the second trip. This time the financial loss was $250. The last of the bankroll from the trail drive now gone, Sam, Joel, and Jack decided to try stage robbery to get some quick cash. Joel planned the scheme, and then a gang was formed of Bass, Collins, Davis, Jim Berry, Bill Heffridge, Tom Nixon, Frank Towle, and Robert "Little Reddy" McKimie. In the first holdup on March 25, 1877, Bass, Collins, Towle, and McKimie hit the stage from Cheyenne when it was about two-and-a-half miles out of Deadwood.

It was a disaster. When the gang attempted to stop the stage coach the horses became frightened and broke into a run. McKimie raised his shotgun, fired, and Johnny Slaughter, the driver, tumbled off dead. The stage, driverless and carrying $15,000, continued on but was soon brought under control by another person on board. McKimie was turned out of the gang for the killing and never rejoined it.

The next holdup succeeded. The gang robbed a stage making the run between Deadwood and various mining camps. It is not known how the desperadoes split up the eleven dollars they took. After a few more petty holdups Towle left the gang to join another that he hoped would be more successful. He was killed a few months later while holding up a stage.

By late August, 1877, the gang, with various com-

Deadwood, Dakota Territory, was a den of thieves, gamblers, and easy women.

binations of members, had held up seven stages. They had almost no luck in picking those carrying gold. On the Cheyenne Trail they got $30, but charitably handed back a dollar to each of the four passengers when they complained at being left penniless.

The gang, now six strong, at last decided to try train robbery. After Berry told them of large gold shipments on the Union Pacific, they struck out for Ogallala, an area Collins knew well. Collins was undisputed leader of the gang at this time, and he set down the plans for the robbery. He fixed the holdup site at the water station at Big Springs, several miles out of Ogallala.

On September 18, 1877, the Number 4 Express was due at Big Springs at 10:48 p.m. Half an hour before the train was due, the gang entered the station office where George Barnhart, the agent and telegrapher, was on duty. They forced him to tear out the telegraph key, cutting off communications. The gang then ordered Barnhart to put a red light out by the track so the train would stop.

When the train halted, Collins and Heffridge ordered the engineer and the fireman off and brought them to the platform, where Berry and Nixon were guarding the conductor; the news agent, W. F. Erdman, was told to remain aboard.

Bass and Davis took the station agent with them through the train until the express car. As usual, the car was locked to protect its cargo of mail, currency, freight, and other valuables. The agent told the express messenger that he had some freight, and he opened up. Once inside, Bass and Davis were joined by Collins and

Heffridge. They got $60,000 in 1877 mintage twenty-dollar gold pieces from three wax-sealed wooden boxes, but they were foiled by the time-lock on the safe, even though Sam attacked it with an axe. The safe contained $200,000. Leaving the express car they went through the train, relieving the passengers of some $1,300.

After waving on the train, the gang buried the loot by the South Platte River and rode into Ogallala as if nothing had happened. Seeing that they were not suspected of the robbery, they returned to where the money was hidden and divided it up, $10,000 going to each man. Bass and Davis then went to Fort Worth, where they split up, Davis going on to South America. Nixon departed for Canada and was not seen again, while Berry went to his home near Mexico, Missouri. Once there, he did some bragging and spent his money freely, drawing the attention of the law. On Sunday, October 14, he was shot and killed while hiding out in the woods. Collins and Heffridge were later killed near Buffalo Station, Kansas, where they had the bad luck to run into some soldiers coming from the opposite direction to look for them for their part in the robbery.

From Fort Worth Bass doubled back to Denton, where he picked up again with Henry Underwood. They were joined by Frank Jackson, and the trio rode down to San Antonio for some fun. But before they got there they learned that three men—a Pinkerton detective and two peace officers—were on their trail, so they moved on toward Fort Worth instead.

On the way they held up a stage, getting $43 for their efforts. The following day Bass and Jackson headed into Denton County, while Underwood went home to spend the holidays with his family. He arrived on Christmas Eve. The next morning a sheriff and his posse, believing Underwood to be Nixon (who was being sought for the Big Springs train robbery), took him into custody. Despite his insistence that he was not Nixon, Underwood could not convince his captors. He was jailed at Kearney, Nebraska, where he stayed until he escaped in March 1878.

A few weeks after Underwood's arrest, Bass and Jackson robbed another stage, getting about $400 and four gold watches. Although this was a fair haul, Bass felt that they should give up on the stages and try a train again. He set about recruiting a new gang, bringing into it Seaborn Barnes, who had been acquitted of a shooting when he was seventeen, and Tom Spotswood, a four-time murderer.

An unknown artist's version of the Sam Bass gang robbing the Houston and Texas Central express car.

The new gang hit the Houston and Texas Central Express at Allen, Texas, on February 22. Boarding the train without difficulty, they ran into trouble when they ordered the express car messenger to open up. He pulled his pistol and both sides started shooting, but no one was hurt. The plucky messenger finally gave in when the outlaws, who had had the foresight to uncouple the car from the rest of the train, threatened to set it, and him, on fire. The gang rode off with about $3,000. But Spotswood had failed to wear a mask during the holdup, and five days later a posse led by the messenger, who had recognized him, arrested him at his ranch. Sentenced to ten years in prison, Spotswood soon won a new trial in a friendlier court on the grounds of "newly discovered evidence," and was acquitted.

Meanwhile, the three other members of the gang were not idle. On March 18 they hit the Houston and Texas Central Express again, this time at Hutchins, not far from Dallas. They first made prisoners of the two men working at the railroad station. Then, as the train slowed for its stop they jumped aboard and covered the engineer and fireman with their guns. Again the express car messenger proved troublesome by shooting it out rather than surrendering. He was wounded in the flurry of gunfire and finally gave in. Bass, Jackson, and Barnes rode off with a small amount of cash. The messenger had the presence of mind to hide the larger share in a stove before he was overpowered.

On March 31 Henry Underwood rejoined the gang, bringing "Arkansaw" Johnson, who had been in jail with him in Kearney. But the gang did not remain at full strength for long. Jackson left to try "going straight"; Barnes fell ill; and Underwood, fresh from prison, wanted to spend some time with his family before going back into full-time action.

All this was fine with Bass, who was planning another train robbery, for if most of his men were seen elsewhere during the time of the next strike, he might not be suspected of pulling it off.

Sam, Arkansaw Johnson, and two "novices" hit a Texas and Pacific train at Eagle Ford on April 4. It was a snap.

As usual, they first captured the station agent, then stopped the train, and marched to the express car. When the messenger refused to open up, Sam broke down the door. There was no shooting this time, and the four men got away easily. But once again the pickings were poor—about $50. The two "novices" took their share and vanished, while Sam and Arkansaw went to Dallas for some relaxation.

Although Sam and his gang had not yet been positively identified as the train robbers, suspicions were strong and widespread. The citizens of Denton County criticized the lawmen for their slowness in making arrests, and Sam must have known time was running out. Nevertheless, he wanted to pull another robbery, hoping to repeat his one notable success at Big Springs. The target was the Mesquite Station of the Texas and Pacific, about twelve miles east of Dallas. The gang— consisting of Bass, Underwood, Jackson, Johnson, Sam Pipes, and Al Herndon—met at the home of Bill Collins to make their plans.

All except Collins went to the Mesquite Station on April 18, 1878. They captured the station agent and, as the train pulled to a halt, the conductor, Jules Alvord, swung down to find himself facing a gun. Instead of obeying a command to raise his hands, he turned and jumped back into the car, grabbed a six-shooter, smashed a window, and started shooting.

In the exchange of gunfire Alvord was hit in the arm and quit the fight. The express car messenger, backed up by a guard with a shotgun, refused Sam's demand that they open up and answered instead with gunfire. Sam went for some kerosene, splashed it on the car, and gave the men inside a count of fifty to change their minds. He got to forty when the door opened. The safe, however, yielded only $150.

The gang separated, but Pipes and Herndon were soon caught and taken to Tyler, Texas, to stand trial. Then, on April 29, Sheriff Everheart of Grayson County learned that Bass and the others were hiding out at Jim Murphy's house in Cove Hollow. Everheart approached with a squad of Rangers, but Bass, on familiar ground, decided to advance to the edge of a canyon dividing the two forces and fight. This time the outlaw came close to losing his life, for during the course of the shooting one bullet severed his cartridge belt and another smashed the rifle he was holding. Bass and the others pulled out, even though they had to leave several of their horses behind. Crossing the canyon delayed the sheriff's pursuit, and even then rough and unfamiliar country prevented the posse from closing in. Nevertheless, the Rangers kept on the outlaws' trail. The gang rode to Henry Underwood's place, then abandoned it when the posse drew near. Then on to Clear Creek; then to Hard Carter's ranch, not far from Denton. The next morning, while the outlaws were eating breakfast, they found themselves surrounded. A fierce gun battle broke out, but the gang faded into the surrounding woods unhurt. Word quickly spread that Bass and his men were hiding nearby and soon the area was full of armed riders looking for action. The gang, however, made their way to the Hickory Creek area and then slipped away.

Late in May they were spotted and surrounded at Big Caddo Creek in Stephens County, but they got out of the trap. On June 5 Bass and his men rode into Denton. Early the next morning they made their way to Work's livery stable and took back their confiscated horses that the Rangers had left at the stable.

A posse gathered and rode out in pursuit. The outlaws were spotted at Clear Creek, but again they got away to be overtaken next at Pilot Knob, some six miles south of Denton, where a gun battle began. The outlaw band kept moving, finally reaching open prairie. The running fight continued throughout the day and into the next. Twice they were surrounded but broke free, finally reaching Salt Creek, in Wise County, an area thick with trees, gullies, and ravines.

On the afternoon of June 12 Rangers came upon the gang camped alongside a stream. A fight started and Johnson was shot through the heart. Bass ordered the rest to scatter and although their horses were captured, the gang escaped. During the night they stole some horses and fled the area. Underwood took this opportunity to desert Bass, and he was not heard from again.

Meanwhile, Jim Murphy and his father had been arrested on May 1 for harboring the outlaws after the Mesquite robbery. Following his arrest Murphy approached Major John B. Jones of the Texas Rangers with a plan for Bass's capture in exchange for having the cases against him and his father dismissed. The bargain was agreed to and on May 21, according to plan, Murphy jumped bond. He made his way home and waited for Bass to contact him. Bass was slow in showing up, mainly because of the battles he had been running with the Rangers, but on June 15 he and Jackson arrived at Murphy's house.

Murphy pretended to throw in with Bass, and the trio then rode out to get Seaborn Barnes. The four-man gang moved on looking out for the next target, a bank. On the way, Henry Collins, along with two strangers, brought word to Bass that Murphy was said to be a traitor. Confronted, Murphy confessed to the plot, but claimed that he agreed to it only so that he would be set free. The outlaws argued over Murphy's fate. Sam decided to kill Murphy, but at the last minute Jackson intervened, still believing in Murphy's loyalty.

The four men passed through a number of towns looking over banks. Murphy suggested that the Williamson County Bank at Round Rock would be a good target, and all hands agreed. During the ride they stopped briefly in Belton and Georgetown, giving Murphy his chance to send word back to Major Jones about the impending strike at Round Rock.

Reaching Round Rock on Sunday, July 14, the gang

pitched camp outside the town and spent the following days making their plans. It was agreed to hit the bank at about 3:30 p.m. the following Saturday. They would approach the bank on foot, having hitched their horses in a nearby alley. Bass and Barnes would enter the bank while Jackson and Murphy guarded the door. Barnes was to ask for change for a five-dollar bill, and when the cashier went to comply, Bass would pull his pistol.

Meanwhile, Murphy's letters had done their work. Round Rock was no longer the quiet little town it seemed to the casual onlooker, nor was the bank "too easy to talk about." Two detachments of Texas Rangers, one under Lt. Reynolds and the other under Lt. Arnold, were already in the area. Major Jones, along with Maurice Moore, deputy sheriff of Travis County, were also there. Jones alerted the bank to get ready, and men were stationed at the railroad depot.

Friday evening the four outlaws set out to get some tobacco at Henry Koppel's general store. Murphy left the group, saying that he was going to buy some corn for the horses.

Bass, Barnes, and Jackson rode into Round Rock and dismounted. As they walked the short distance toward the store, Deputy Sheriff Moore spotted them; he hurried to Deputy Sheriff Grimes of Williamson County, who stood nearby. Moore had not recognized the trio but he had noticed the bulge of a pistol under a coat. "I think one of those men has a six-shooter on," Moore said to Grimes. The two deputies crossed the street and entered the store behind the outlaws. Moore stood by the door as Grimes walked up to Bass and asked if he was wearing a gun. According to Moore's account,

They all three replied, "Yes," and at the same instant two of them shot Grimes and one shot me [through the lungs].

After I had fired my first shot, I could not see the men on account of the smoke. They continued shooting, and so did I, until I fired five shots. As they passed out [of the store], I saw one man bleeding from the arm and side; I then leaned against the store door, feeling faint and sick, and recovering myself, I started on and fired the remaining shot at one of them.

Having lent one of my pistols to another man the day before, I stopped and reloaded my pistol, went into the stable, and got my Winchester and started in pursuit of them, and was stopped by Dr. Morris, who said, "Hold on; don't go any further, for if you get overheated your wound may kill you." I stopped and gave my Winchester to another man. Grimes did not have time to pull out his pistol; six bullet holes were put through his body.

The Rangers, hearing the firing, came upon the scene and fired upon the robbers as they retreated. Major Jones reached the place in time to engage in the fusillade. The whole village was thrown into a tumult of excitement, and the citizens, who could procure arms, joined in the affray. The *robbers taking cover behind houses and fences, and firing back at every opportunity, retreated down an alley towards their horses. Early in the engagement Bass had received a shot through the hand, and as they retreated down the alley, a Ranger, George Harrall, shot him in the back, inflicting a mortal wound. He [Bass], however, reached and mounted his horse. [Actually, Bass was helped on his horse by Jackson, who held the wounded man in the saddle as they rode away.] Barnes was shot by Geo. Ware, a Ranger, through the head, just as he mounted his horse, and fell dead on the spot. Jackson and Bass rode off together. Major Jones, Ware, and Tubbs fired at them as they left. F. L. Jordan and Albert Highsmith, citizens of Round Rock, joined in the fight and did their best to lift the robbers out of their saddles. Major Jones, Captain Lee Hall, and three Rangers gave chase on horseback, but the bandits had the start of them too far, and they lost the trail and returned to town. That evening Lieutenant Reynolds with ten Rangers, from San Saba, and Lieutenant Armstrong, from Austin, with a squad, arrived at Round Rock. After Bass and Jackson had gone several miles from the scene, Bass's wounds began to grow so sore that he found he would have to stop. Jackson wanted to stop and remain with him, but Bass told him no—that he was seriously wounded and must stop, and that Frank must take care of himself. He gave Jackson all the money he had, his horse, arms, and am-*

munition and enjoined him to go and leave him. Jackson took his departure from Bass and left him there alone. After Jackson left, Bass went to a house to get some water. He was bloody and looked very feeble; this attracted the attention of the lady of the house who gave him the water. After he got the water, he left afoot and the lady saw the direction he went. Next morning she informed his pursuers of the incident and by this means he was found.

That morning a small party of Rangers discovered Bass lying under a tree about four miles from town. Although he was brought back to town and treated for his wounds, Bass's injuries were fatal, and he rapidly lost strength. Repeatedly questioned about the gang's activities, he refused to give any helpful details. Of the Round Rock shooting, Bass had this to say: "Grimes asked if I had a pistol. Said I had, and then all three of us drew and shot him. If I killed him, he was the first man I ever killed." Sam Bass died the following day, July 21, 1878.

BILLY
THE
KID

VIRTUALLY NOTHING IS KNOWN ABOUT THE EARLY LIFE of Billy the Kid. His birthplace and date, although usually reported as New York City, November 23, 1859, are not authenticated and may be wrong. It is known that his real name was Henry McCarty. His father is said to have died when the boy was only three years old.

On May 1, 1873, his mother, Mrs. Catherine Mc-Carty, married her second husband, William Henry Harrison Antrim, in the First Presbyterian Church, Santa Fe, New Mexico. Henry and his older brother Joe were witnesses.

Just how long the McCartys had been in Santa Fe is unknown, but very soon after the wedding the family moved to Silver City, New Mexico. Henry's mother died from tuberculosis about eighteen months later on September 16, 1874, at the age of forty-five.

When Henry was sixteen he got into his first scrape

with the law. He was arrested and jailed for stealing some clothes from two Chinese, Charley Sun and Sam Chung. He escaped from jail soon after by climbing out through the chimney.

Henry was not heard of again until August, 1877, when he showed up at Fort Grant, Arizona. Here, on the 17th, he shot a blacksmith named E. P. "Windy" Cahill. According to one story, Cahill was a big, blustery man who liked to bully people. He had taken to shoving Henry around, and on this particular day he threw the boy to the floor of Adkin's saloon, pinned his arms with his knees and slapped him. The boy managed to reach his gun and shot Cahill. He died the following day.

During this period the boy was known by several names—Henry McCarty, Henry Antrim, and Kid Antrim. He soon dropped them all. Instead, he took the William H. from his stepfather, and added Bonney—no one knows why. Through the rest of his short life he would have the nickname Billy the Kid.

Fearful of arrest, Billy drifted from Fort Grant into New Mexico. Motherless and homeless—his stepfather had been unable or unwilling to take care of him—and with murder and a petty theft hanging over his head, Billy kept moving. For a while he tried his hand at horse stealing with Jesse Evans and his gang, then operating in the Territory of New Mexico. Evans and his men, however, soon headed back to their home base in Lincoln County. Billy went on alone to Mesilla, Texas. Here, in September, 1877, he was reported to have been one of a party that stole some horses from a coal camp in the Burro Mountains. True or not, Billy fled before he could be arrested, making for Lincoln County where he visited with Evans' bunch. From the Evans camp he went on to see Jim Dolan of the L. G. Murphy & Company outfit, with whom he stayed for a few days. He soon got into a squabble with Billy Morton, Dolan's foreman, and he pulled out.

Billy later turned up at George Coe's ranch some seventy miles away. There he met J. H. Tunstall, an English rancher and merchant, and Alexander McSween, a Lincoln lawyer and rancher. These two men had opened a store and a bank, backed by the powerful cattleman, John Chisum. The establishment of this business triggered a series of events culminating in "the Lincoln County War."

Before Tunstall and McSween went into business, L. G. Murphy & Company had flourished as an economic and political power in the county. No small measure of the firm's wealth was due to the highly profitable practice of buying cattle, stolen from Chisum, and selling the beef under contract to the Army at Fort Stanton and to the Mescalero Apache Reservation.

Ex-Army officers Lawrence G. Murphy and Emil Fritz had been partners in this enterprise. Fritz went back to his native Germany on a visit and died there in 1874, leaving $10,000 in insurance to his heirs: a brother and sister. The policy was turned over to McSween to collect, which he did, charging over $4,000 for expenses and services.

After the death of Fritz, Jim Dolan became an active partner, and John Riley (who had invested an inheritance in the firm) became a junior partner of the Murphy operation, which was a monopoly too powerful for any individual to challenge. But when McSween and Tunstall opened their store and bank in 1877, in direct competition with Dolan, Riley and Murphy, people began to choose sides. Some of the smaller ranchers, who resented Chisum's power, took the growing feud as an opportunity to "get even," and thus put their chips on Murphy. Others, some of whom wanted to see the Murphy economic stranglehold broken, sided with Chisum.

Hatred smoldered and positions became fixed. Only a small spark was needed to light the fuse.

Then, on January 26, 1878, Tunstall wrote a letter to the *Mesilla Independent,* publicly accusing the Murphy group of stealing county tax money. The fuse began to burn.

McSween, meanwhile, continued to refuse to come through with what remained of the $10,000 in insurance money. A writ of attachment was issued against the Tunstall-McSween property. Still refusing to pay, McSween was indicted for embezzlement and a warrant went out for his arrest.

McSween hired gunmen to protect himself from arrest. Murphy, in turn, added men to his forces. On February 18 Sheriff Brady—a Dolan-faction man—sent a posse to serve Tunstall with the writ of attachment.

That same day Tunstall, with his foreman, Dick Brewer, and John Middleton, Bob Widenmann, and Billy the Kid, left the Tunstall ranch to move a band of horses legally exempt from the attachment order. Late that afternoon Billy and Middleton dropped back from the band about five hundred yards to chase after some wild turkeys and, some distance ahead, Brewer and Widenmann drifted off the trail. Tunstall was riding alone.

Suddenly Brady's posse, eighteen men strong, rode over the crest of a hill and, guns firing, quickly surrounded Tunstall. They drove Billy the Kid and the others to cover on a nearby hill, where they found themselves powerless to help Tunstall. Forced off his horse, Tunstall was shot through the chest by Jesse Evans. Billy Morton then took Tunstall's own pistol, killed him with a shot through the head and the posse rode off.

Later, Billy the Kid and another of Tunstall's men, Fred Waite, went to Lincoln and made sworn statements against the murderers. The warrants were given to Constable Martinez, who took Billy and Fred along to Dolan's store to help serve the papers. But before they could enter to see if any of Tunstall's killers were present they were met by Sheriff Brady. He turned the tables by arresting all three for "disturbing the peace," freeing the constable later in the day but holding Billy and Fred until after Tunstall's funeral. Immediately following the funeral, Tunstall's friends held a meeting. They formed themselves into a group called the Regulators, with Dick Brewer at its head. Brewer, backed up with the title of special constable and holding warrants for the arrest of the Tunstall killers, rode out with the Regulators on March 2 to begin the hunt.

There were eleven in the group, including Billy. The following day they came upon Billy Morton, Frank Baker, and three others resting under a tree. The five men grabbed their horses and galloped off with the Regulators close behind. Morton and Baker were finally taken; the other three escaped. The Regulators took the prisoners to Chisum's headquarters on March 8, and the next day they began the long ride to Lincoln. According to Frank McNab, one of the Regulators, after riding about twenty miles Morton suddenly snatched a pistol from one of the riders and killed him. Morton and Baker then made a break for freedom, but they were overtaken and killed. Other reports suggested that the two captives were murdered in cold blood. Regardless of what really happened, three men were dead.

The Regulators broke into two groups and went into hiding for several weeks. At the end of the month Billy and five others drifted back to Lincoln.

On Monday, April 1, Sheriff Brady, George Hindman, Billy Matthews, Jack Long, and George Peppin walked down the street on their way to put up a postponement notice about the opening of court. Billy and his friends saw the sheriff's group, and perhaps thinking that they were coming after them, hid behind a plank corral gate jutting out from the rear of Tunstall's store. As Brady and his men passed the front of the store and came in line with the rear gate the gang opened fire. Brady fell dead and Hindman was mortally wounded.

The Regulators rode into the hills where they joined up with Brewer and the others. Their strength was increased further with the arrival of Tom O'Folliard, from

Uvalde, Texas, who soon became Billy's closest friend. On April 4 the Regulators moved on to Doc Blazer's place, where they could get a meal and bed down for the night. While the men were resting up outside before dinner, they spotted a rider coming toward the house on a mule. Frank Coe, one of the Regulators, recognized the man as "Buckshot" Roberts, one of the men in the group that killed Tunstall. Roberts was at this point a bounty hunter, seeking a reward of $200 for the arrest of each of the men in on the Brady and Hindman killings. He had been told in Lincoln that Billy the Kid. Brewer, and some others might be found in the vicinity of Blazer's Mill.

Coe met Roberts and told him that his life might be spared if he surrendered peacefully. The two men sat down on the steps of the house to talk things over. But the other men, keeping out of sight, grew itchy. They pulled their guns and came into view. Charlie Bowdre spoke first, demanding that Roberts surrender. Roberts refused. Both men fired at once—Bowdre's bullet tearing into Roberts' stomach. Roberts, because of an old buckshot wound—the source of his nickname—could not raise his rifle to his shoulder to aim and fire. Firing from his lap, the bullet hit Bowdre's gun belt buckle and ricochetted into George Coe's hand, severing his trigger finger.

Roberts, although mortally wounded, fired again, putting a bullet through Middleton's lung. He kept firing, driving the Kid and the others back to safety. Roberts then staggered into Blazer's bedroom, where

Billy the Kid.

he found a 50-caliber Buffalo gun. He set himself up by a window and prepared for a long fight.

The stunned Regulators withdrew to figure out what to do next. Brewer made his way to a nearby sawmill, where he thought he would have a clear shot. He fired once but missed; so did Roberts' answering bullet. There was a lull, then suddenly Roberts opened up with the Buffalo gun, and Brewer fell dead, the top of his head gone.

The rest of the band decided to quit the fight. Coe needed help, and Middleton was in poor shape. They went away, leaving the dying Roberts in Blazer's care.

In the months that followed, the Murphy bunch vigorously harried the McSween faction. Billy the Kid and the others, meanwhile, had returned to the area around Lincoln. With fairly strong forces available, McSween decided to put everything into one big attempt to seize control of Lincoln itself. And so, on the night of July 14, 1878, McSween's men slipped into the small settlement and took up positions: nine Mexicans in the Montana house; fifteen—McSween, Billy the Kid, Harvey Morris, José Chávez y Chávez, Yginio Salazar, Florencio Chaves, Ignacio Gonzales, Vincente Romero, Francisco Zamora, Jim French, Tom O'Folliard, José Maria Sánchez, Joe Smith, Tom Cullins, and George Bowers—in the McSween house; three—Henry Brown, George Coe, and Sam Smith—in a warehouse behind the Tunstall building; a dozen or so—including Charlie Bowdre, Josiah Scurlock, John Middleton, "Dirty Steve" Stevens, among others—in the Isaac Ellis home; and five men in the Patron house.

The McSween forces, though deployed in considerable force, were widely separated. But most important, they were for the most part entrenched in defensive rather than offensive positions. This tactical error proved costly.

Lincoln's Sheriff Peppin, a Dolan man, was caught by surprise when the presence of McSween's forces became known. He spread his men out as well as he could and sent for Deputy Sheriff William B. Powell, who was in nearby San Patricio. Reinforcements arrived the next morning, bringing Peppin's force to nearly thirty men.

The sheriff had warrants for Billy the Kid, Brown, Scurlock, and Bowdre, on murder charges, and one for McSween for embezzlement. But when his men tried to serve the papers, gunfire drove them off.

The first day passed in relative quiet, except for the death of a local citizen—allegedly poisoned by a relative because he had been friendly with the McSween faction.

On July 16, Peppin wrote to Lt. Col. N. A. M. Dudley, commanding Fort Stanton, asking to borrow a howitzer. Although Dudley refused the request, he let it be known that he was in sympathy with the Murphy side. A Private Robinson took Dudley's written reply to Lincoln, but as he neared the plaza he was fired on. Peppin promptly wrote Dudley that his soldier had been shot at by the McSween group.

July 17 passed with one man killed and three wounded, and on July 18 George Bowers was wounded and Tom Cullins was killed.

Dudley decided to move troops into Lincoln "for the preservation of the lives of the women and children, and in response to the numerous petitions received from persons in that town. . . ." On the morning of July 19 he arrived in the plaza with five officers, leading a contingent of thirty-five soldiers, a howitzer and a Gatling gun. Camping about 300 yards from the McSween home and thirty yards from the Patron place, he then announced to both sides that he had not come to assist either one. His very presence, however, revived the rather dispirited Murphy side and discouraged the McSween group.

Dudley had the Justice of the Peace issue a warrant for McSween's arrest for the attempted murder of Private Robinson. Peppin deputized Bob Beckwith and ordered him to serve the warrant.

Later in the morning more than a dozen men, led by Deputy Sheriff Turner, rushed the McSween house, fired through the front windows, and pulled back without harm. At one-thirty in the afternoon one man reached the house, poured coal oil on the floor of one of the two kitchens, and started a fire. It died out after a short time. A second attempt was made, this time by lighting shaving chips and kindling by the back door of the northwest kitchen. This fire caught. It soon burned along one side, across the front, and back up the other side. Then there was an explosion inside, and the house blazed even more furiously.

The only room untouched by the fire at that point was the northeast kitchen—opposite the one in which the fire began. The men inside gathered there to plan their next move. To remain was to die. George Bowers, who had been seriously wounded on July 18, chose death by fire. The others decided to make a break for it.

Soon after dark they raced from the house in two groups—Billy the Kid, Chávez y Chávez, French, O'Folliard, and Morris in the first group. Morris was killed as he reached the fence gate near the east side of the building. The others made it to safety.

McSween and the others made up the second bunch. They headed for the fence gate on the north side, but intense gunfire drove them back in the yard between a woodpile and the chicken house. They were trapped. Two of the Mexicans, possibly Romero and Zamora, hid in the chicken house; the rest took shelter behind the woodpile.

It was a hopeless situation, and McSween offered to surrender to Beckwith. Beckwith, with three others, stepped forward, and at that moment a shot rang out from the chicken house, killing him; in the return fire McSween fell dead on top of Beckwith. In the confusion some of the McSween men in this second group made a break for it. Salazar was hit twice, but crawled away later that night. The others made it safely. The two men in the chicken house were called on to surrender; when they refused they were killed.

Thus the battle ended. The McSween forces were beaten and scattered. The Murphy victory was, in the end, a hollow one. Alliances dissolved, bitterness and suspicion wrought havoc in the county, and virtual anarchy ensued. The violence and the lawlessness were to continue for a long time.

Several days later the McSween-faction survivors gathered again, joined by Waite, Bowdre, and Middleton. Billy the Kid assumed leadership of the ragged band, and it moved on.

On August 5 the Kid, Henry Brown, George Coe, and six or eight Mexicans set out to try to find the burial place of their friend Dick Brewer. On the way they stopped near the Mescalero Apache Indian Agency. The Mexicans watered their horses, while Billy, Brown, and Coe went to get a drink of water from a spring. The bookkeeper at the Indian Agency, Morris J. Bernstein, probably suspected that the riders were Regulators on the prowl, for while Billy and the others were at the spring Bernstein and some Indians suddenly attacked the Mexicans. The bookkeeper himself was killed by Atanacio Martinez, one of the Mexicans, but it was widely assumed that the Kid had done it, and the story spread that he and his group had been stealing horses when Bernstein tried to stop them.

The little band kept moving, the Mexicans going their own way. Billy, with O'Folliard, Waite, Brown, and Middleton, headed for the area around Fort Sumner. Bowdre, who was married, decided to go to his wife, and so left the gang temporarily.

The group continued on to Bosque Grande, the old Chisum headquarters, on August 13. From there they rode with Chisum's men to Sumner with a herd of cattle, the Kid and his men then moving on to Tascosa with some stolen horses. They sold the horses and stayed around awhile and relaxed until the money was gone and it was time to move on once again. Middleton,

Brown, and Waite decided to go their own way, leaving only Billy and Tom to travel back to Fort Sumner for some gambling and horse racing.

That December they returned to Lincoln. The following February 18 a meeting was arranged between Billy and Tom and the Murphy faction represented by Dolan and Campbell to end the still smoldering feud. The meeting was an apparent success, for when it was over everyone was roaring drunk except Billy, who, being a teetotaler, abstained. The four men went off together to continue drinking at the Cullen saloon. On the way they ran into a lawyer named Chapman who, in response to their wisecracks, told them to mind their own business. Chapman paid with his life for this show of backbone; Dolan and Bill Campbell shot him down in the street and went on to the saloon as if nothing had happened. At the first opportunity Tom and the Kid slipped away. Because of the mood Dolan and Campbell were in, Billy knew his turn would have been next.

Billy and Tom were declared material witnesses to the Chapman murder and warrants were issued for their arrest. A month later, on March 17, Billy held a secret meeting with Governor Lew Wallace in Lincoln. The governor offered him amnesty if the Kid would testify against the killers. Billy agreed, and he and Tom were arrested voluntarily. After testifying before a grand jury about the Chapman affair, Billy waited for his own case—the charge of murdering Sheriff Brady—to come up. According to the deal with the governor, the case would be thrown out and he would be released. But something went wrong. The prosecuting attorney refused to withdraw the murder charge and Billy was held under a fairly loose house arrest until formal proceedings could begin. O'Folliard was held on another charge. On June 17, 1879, they both escaped and, joined by Doc Scurlock and Charlie Bowdre, went to Fort Sumner to gamble and play the horses.

While at the Fort, Billy sometimes visited with a man named Pat Garrett, who ran a bar and restaurant. They became casual friends as the summer passed pleasantly and quietly.

That October the Kid stole some of Chisum's steers and sold them to cover part of what the cattleman had promised but never paid Billy and the others for serving in the Lincoln County War. Soon after this Scurlock decided to pull up stakes, leaving only the Kid, Tom, and Charlie together.

In January of 1880 the three of them went into Bob Hargrove's saloon in Lincoln. There Joe Grant, a man who had been loudly boasting that he would kill Billy the Kid, was drunkenly toying with another man's fancy pearl-handled six-shooter. Billy admired the gun and asked to see it. While handling it, he noticed an empty chamber in the cylinder, and before he returned it to Grant he turned the cylinder so that the empty chamber was next in line. When Grant thought the time was right, he turned the gun on Billy and pulled the trigger. Billy, in "self-defense," pulled his own gun and killed Grant.

The Kid spent the next few months gambling and probably working at horse stealing. He rode the circuit between Sumner, Anton Chico, White Oaks, and Sumner again. At Anton Chico he got to know Jim Greathouse, a Texan who ran a freighting business. Jim numbered among his friends a number of outlaws from Las Vegas, including Dave Rudebaugh, Billie Wilson, and Tom Pickett. They all soon became close friends of the Kid.

Meanwhile, Pat Garrett had been appointed a deputy sheriff. Billy still had a federal indictment open against him for the Roberts killing, and he, O'Folliard, and Bowdre also faced the Brady murder charge. Although the Kid and Garrett had been friendly, they were now, with Pat's appointment, on opposing sides. Pressure began to mount for Garrett to "do something" about the Kid.

Billy decided to talk to Judge Leonard, the lawyer for Mrs. McSween, in the hope that he would take the Kid's case to the governor. A new prosecuting attorney was to be named soon; maybe the governor could get this one to drop the indictments.

The Kid rode to White Oaks with Rudebaugh and Wilson, stealing some horses on the way. They lay over for a few days at Greathouse's stage station and got rid of the horses. On November 20 they went on to White Oaks but found that the judge was then in Lincoln. The trio stayed briefly at the West & Dedrick livery stable and corrals at the edge of White Oaks, then made camp about five miles away near Coyote Spring at an abandoned sawmill But there was to be no peace. Their presence was reported, and the next morning a nine-man posse rode out to the sawmill. After a brief gunfight the Kid, Dave, and Billie returned to the Greathouse station.

Several days later the posse, now thirteen strong, rode up near the station where they grabbed Joe Steck, the camp cook. Steck was given a note demanding the outlaws' surrender and told to deliver it. The men in the station wrote back asking for a chance to talk with the posse's leader, Jim Carlyle. But once inside Carlyle was made a hostage. At about eleven o'clock that night the posse decided to storm the building, and word was sent for both Steck and Greathouse's partner, Mr. Cook —who had been carrying messages while Steck took care of dinner—to clear out of the house.

Just as the two men stepped outside, Carlyle panicked. He crashed through a window and made a run for it. A flurry of shots rang out and he fell dead. Steck and Cook made their way to the posse, where they learned that Carlyle had been killed by his own men, who thought that Steck and Cook were decoys covering the escape of the outlaws, and opened fire when Carlyle crashed out of the house.

With their leader dead, the posse withdrew, and the trio left the station safely.

In early December Billy, Bowdre, O'Folliard, Pickett, Rudebaugh, and Wilson showed up at Fort Sumner again. Here Billy learned that Governor Wallace had offered $500 for the arrest of "William Bonney and his delivery to the sheriff of Lincoln County. . . ."

Garrett, Barney Mason, and Frank Stewart left Las Vegas for Anton Chico on December 14 on the trail of the Kid, and were joined by six more men before they reached Fort Sumner. But Billy and his friends had pulled out. Four days later Garrett hid his men while he and another man walked around the town, showing themselves. As he hoped, word went out to Billy that Garrett was at Sumner—and that he had almost no help. A note rigged by Garrett was delivered to the Kid, reporting that Garrett and his small party had left town.

The ruse worked. That night Billy's gang rode back into Fort Sumner. As they turned the corner of the old Indian Hospital building the trap was sprung. O'Folliard was hit and mortally wounded by the first blast of gunfire from the concealed posse. Tom was captured but lived only a few moments.

Billy believed that Garrett and his men had left town.

The rest of the outlaws got away, making it to the Wilcox & Brazil ranch. Brazil was sent to Sumner to look things over. Unknown to Billy, Brazil was Garrett's friend and when he reached Sumner he told Garrett where to find Billy and the other four. Garrett sent him back, hoping to trap the outlaws with another ruse, but they had already fled. The posse tracked the Kid and his men to Stinking Springs, where there was an unused stone shack in which the outlaws were holed up. Garrett's men hid near the shack during the night. At dawn, when Bowdre came out to feed the horses, Garrett shouted "Hands Up!" then both he and Lee Hall fired, hitting Bowdre in the chest.

Billy pulled Charlie back inside and saw that he was dying. He took Bowdre's pistol and placed it in the bleeding man's hand, telling him to go on out and get the posse-men. Bowdre staggered outside, collapsed and died. The Kid and the others were trapped inside throughout the bitterly cold day. Late that afternoon the posse started cooking supper. The smell of it was too much. The outlaws, frozen and half starved, surrendered. It was two days before Christmas.

They were taken by wagon to the Wilcox ranch, where they remained overnight. The next day they went on to Fort Sumner, then to Las Vegas. From there they traveled by train to Santa Fe, where they were jailed on the evening of December 27.

Billy was brought to Mesilla to stand trial. His first case was called on April 6, 1881, for the killing of Roberts. The federal indictment was dismissed when it was shown that Roberts had not been killed on Indian

Agency—that is, government—property but on Dr. Blazer's land—private property, not subject to federal control. The Kid was immediately arrested for the Brady killing. He was convicted of murder in the first degree and sentenced to hang.

He was taken from Mesilla to Lincoln on April 18; the hanging was scheduled for May 13. Arriving in Lincoln on April 21, he was placed in a second floor room of the old Murphy-Dolan store, which had been converted to a courthouse and jail.

Billy was guarded by Deputy Marshal Bob Olinger and Deputy Sheriff J. W. Bell. In mid-afternoon of April 28 Olinger took several prisoners across the street for dinner at Wortley's Hotel. Exactly what happened next has never been agreed upon and may never be known. It may be, as one respectable version has it, that a man named Sam Corbett hid a revolver in the jail's outhouse, then slipped a note to Billy about it. Billy went there while Bell stood guard outside. The Kid found the gun, hid it in his waistband, and when he came out he drew on Bell and marched him upstairs. The deputy suddenly made a break for it. Billy fired at him and missed, but the bullet ricochetted off the stairway wall and hit Bell below the left armpit. He staggered outside and fell dead.

Olinger heard the shot. Thinking that Bell had shot the Kid, he left his prisoners in front of Wortley's and hurried across the street. Billy had by this time armed himself with Olinger's shotgun, which had been left upstairs. As Olinger neared the building Billy called to him from the second floor window. "Hello, Bob," he said. Olinger looked up as Billy let him have one barrel of the double-barreled shotgun.

Billy then got a prospector's pick from Godfrey Gauss, the jail cook, and pried one leg iron loose. Gauss saddled a horse for him, but before mounting the Kid went over to Olinger and fired the second barrel of the shotgun into him.

The Kid eventually made his way back to the country around Fort Sumner, where he remained in hiding. No one can say why he did not leave for Mexico or some other relatively safe place. For several months Garrett seemed uninterested in the Kid's case or reluctant to go after him; perhaps he was preoccupied with other demands. This was Billy's chance to clear out of the territory, but he did not go.

In July word got around that Billy had been seen near the Fort. The news reached Garrett, who was some forty miles away. By now Garrett was feeling the sting of rumors about his failure to get Billy. Pat, who had been elected sheriff on the first of the year, had to go after Billy, no matter how he felt about the Kid. On July 10, Garrett, Deputy Kip McKinney, and John Poe went to Sumner. They had no luck in learning anything about the Kid's whereabouts. Finally, Garrett decided to pay a call on his old friend Pete Maxwell—who also knew Billy—to see if he had any news.

Billy, meanwhile, had been staying at a sheep camp near Maxwell's home, which was located on the grounds of old Fort Sumner. The night of July 14, Billy came into town to visit his girlfriend, Celsa Gutiérrez. She wanted to cook a meal for him, but had no meat. Recalling that Maxwell had a fresh-killed heifer in his ice house, she suggested that Billy get the key to it from Pete. Billy took along a butcher knife to cut off a nice steak.

Garrett had just arrived at Maxwell's place and gone in to talk with him, posting Poe and McKinney outside. Billy walked up and spotted the two men sitting on the edge of the porch. He asked who they were but, getting no immediate response, he went on inside to Maxwell's bedroom to ask for the ice house key and to inquire about the men outside. It was midnight. In the darkness Billy made out the form of a man sitting at the head of Maxwell's bed. Speaking in Spanish, he asked who was there. There was no reply. Now alert to danger, Billy took a step back and repeated his question. This time Garrett recognized the Kid's voice. Without a word Garrett fired his six-shooter twice. The second shot missed, but it did not matter. The first bullet had caught Billy the Kid in the heart.

BLACK BART

BLACK BART, WHOSE REAL NAME WAS PROBABLY
Charles E. Boles, has been described as "the most
famous, most mysterious, and most elusive lone stage
robber ever to operate in the West." The exact dates of
his birth and death are unknown and virtually nothing
is known about his background prior to July 26, 1875.

On that day, John Shine, the driver of a stage running between Sonora and Milton, California, was sur-
prised by a strangely dressed man emerging from
behind a big boulder. The man motioned with a shotgun for the stage to stop. He was dressed in a linen
duster; a flour sack, with cut-outs for the eyes, covered
his head. He wore heavy socks over his shoes.

"Throw down the box!" the lone bandit commanded.
Shine hesitated. The hooded man called, "If he dares
to shoot, give him a solid volley, boys." Looking around,
the driver saw six guns aimed at the stage from
strategic points in the underbrush flanking the road.
He dropped the box to the ground.

The gunman smashed the box with an axe, removed

several bags of gold coins and some express packages, and told Shine to move on. Shine went ahead a short distance, and when he saw that the bandit had disappeared he ran back. He found the empty box. He also discovered that the six "guns" aimed at him from the brush were only carefully placed sticks. Shine went on to Copperopolis, four miles away, to sound the alarm but the posse found no suspect.

From this rather bizarre beginning when he was already in his early forties, Black Bart went on to rob twenty-seven more stagecoaches in eight years.

He always operated alone and never fired his gun. Later he claimed that it was not even loaded. He was inordinately polite, tipping his hat to the ladies and allowing them to keep their jewelry.

Twice he left a poem at the scene of his holdups. The first time marked the occasion of his fourth robbery. On August 3, 1877, Black Bart stepped into the road in front of the stage bound from Fort Ross to Russian River. As usual, he was polite but firm. On command the driver tossed the strong box from the stage and rode on. The outlaw got three hundred dollars in cash and a check for $305.52. Later when a posse arrived at the robbery site, they found the emptied box and a piece of paper on which a poem appeared, each of its lines written differently, perhaps to confuse handwriting analysis later on. It read:

> I've labored long and hard for bread—
> For honor and for riches—
> But on my corns too long you've tred,
> You fine-haired sons of . . . .

As a parting bit of whimsy he signed the name "Black Bart, The Po8." It was not long before someone figured out that "Po8" was PoEight, or Poet.

Black Bart obviously was not the robber's name, nor did the poem provide much of a lead. His disguise was perfect; the only memorable trait of the man himself was a deep, hollow voice. Too, a cryptic postscript was judged to have been written in his natural hand, and it suggested to detectives that the outlaw perhaps held some clerical position.

Following this robbery, Black Bart was not heard of for nearly a year. Then, on July 25, 1878, near Berry Creek, the Quincy to Oroville stage was stopped by a man with a flour sack covering his head. Cradling a shotgun in his arm, the bandit told the driver to throw down the money box. This time the take was $379, plus a diamond ring, a watch, and the mail. The man then faded into the woods. The next day the empty Wells, Fargo box was recovered. Another poem was inside. This one contained twelve lines, the middle four a repetition of the first poem. The rest of the poem read:

Here I lay me down to sleep
To wait the coming morrow
Perhaps success, perhaps defeat
And everlasting sorrow
. . . .
Let come what will, I'll try it on
My condition can't be worse
And if there's money in that box
Tis munny in my purse.

Again it was signed "Black Bart the Po8." It was his last poem.

William Irwin, the Governor of California, posted a $300 reward for Black Bart's capture and conviction; Wells, Fargo added another $300 and the postal authorities $200. But finding any useful clues on the outlaw was not easy. The robberies continued—three more stages over the next seven months. Then he seemed to vanish. Spring gave way to summer before another stage was held up.

Bart, however, was getting careless. He frequently stopped at farms and ranches for food and lodging, although never in his disguise and never giving any hint that he was the now-notorious stagecoach robber. But detectives combing the area of the robberies were on the lookout for any stranger, and the reports began to pile up. At one farm it was learned that a "tourist" had stopped by. There were a few noticeable things about him: a tear in a coatsleeve had been repaired with white thread; his shoes had been split for easier walking; and his broken watch chain was patched with a piece of leather. As for the man himself he was described as having smooth hands, two missing front teeth, blue eyes, and graying brown hair. He seemed, most significantly, to be a gentleman.

Meanwhile, the robberies continued. On September 1, 1880, the Weaverville to Redding stage was held up. The next day a man with graying brown hair and blue eyes stopped by a ranch on Eagle Creek to ask for breakfast. The rancher later recalled that the man was extremely polite.

The rate of stagecoach holdups accelerated: three within the last two months of 1881. A long lull followed. Then, on July 13, 1882, while Black Bart was holding up a stage between Laporte and Oroville, he ran into his first opposition.

It was Bart's twenty-third robbery. After he emptied the box he started off, as usual, on foot. But before he got out of sight the Wells, Fargo messenger grabbed a gun and shot twice in the outlaw's direction. No one knows whether Bart was hit, but it was the first time a shot had been fired on either side.

Pressure increased for his capture. But even armed with an accurate description of Bart—American, five feet eight inches tall, gray hair, moustache and chin whiskers, slender build, age something over fifty, two front teeth missing—the law could not find him.

Then four robberies later, on November 3, 1883, outside of Reynolds Ferry, on the Sonora to San Francisco stage run, Black Bart hailed the stage. The driver was Reason E. McConnell. The only other person on board was Jimmy Rolleri, nineteen years old, who worked on the Reynolds Ferry and was going to Copperopolis. The boy had taken his rifle in hopes of spotting some game along the way. As the stage made its way up a hill Jimmy jumped off, planning to cut through the woods and meet the stage again as it came down the other side of the hill.

When the stage reached the peak, Black Bart stepped into the road, dressed in the familiar duster and sack. This time there was no money box to throw down—it was bolted to the floor of the stage. Bart ordered Mc-

*Black Bart, the "Po8,"
was a dapper, derbied
bandit who
worked alone.*

Connell to unhitch the horses and take them down the road out of sight. The outlaw then proceeded to smash the box with an axe, getting $550 in gold coins, $65 in gold dust, and 228 ounces of amalgam worth $4,200.

As Bart was working on the box, McConnell walked ahead with the horses. Suddenly he spotted Jimmy. He signaled for the boy to meet him farther down the road out of Bart's sight. The two made their plans, then crept back near the stage. Bart had by now finished the job. He stood holding a sack containing the money, and a bundle of papers. McConnell reportedly took Jimmy's rifle and fired twice. According to Jimmy, McConnell missed, and the boy took his turn, wounding Bart with one shot. The bandit dropped the papers but held on to the sack and escaped.

The robbery spot was soon swarming with investigators. They found a derby hat (Bart apparently wore it under his hood), bags of crackers and sugar, and several other items, the most significant of which was a handkerchief bearing the laundry mark F.X.0.7. A hunter reported meeting a man fitting Bart's description not far from the robbery who had asked directions to Jackson. A number of other people had met the man with the moustache, too, and the trail grew warmer.

The tell-tale laundry mark sent detectives combing San Francisco, and on November 12 the laundry was located. The mark belonged to a man who had given his name as C. E. Bolton, a resident of Webb House, a hotel at 37 Second Street.

Bolton was arrested, indignantly protesting his innocence and sticking to his story that he was a mining man and a gentleman. But he finally confessed to one of the robberies—the last—and was sentenced to a six-year term at San Quentin, beginning on November 21, 1883.

Black Bart was released on January 21, 1888. He remained in San Francisco for several weeks, then vanished, never to be seen again. For a time various stages were held up by a lone bandit, and speculation ran high that Black Bart was in action again. Gradually even these speculations faded and Black Bart was no more.

Black Bart was certainly one of the most enigmatic figures in outlaw history. To the end of his prison term he claimed that his name was Bolton and that he had been a captain in the Civil War. Yet in his room in San Francisco, these words were written on the flyleaf of a Bible: "This precious Bible is presented to Charles E. Boles, First Sergeant, Company B, 116th Illinois Volunteer Infantry, by his wife as a New Year's gift. . . ." Bart claimed that the Bible was not his. He admitted only that at the time of his arrest he was fifty years old, and that he had been born in Jefferson County, New York.

BUTCH
CASSIDY
AND THE
WILD BUNCH

GEORGE LEROY PARKER, BETTER KNOWN AS BUTCH
Cassidy, was born in Circle Valley, Utah, in 1867.
Reared on his father's ranch not far from Circleville,
George came to know Mike Cassidy, one of his father's
cowhands who also was a horse thief and cattle rustler
on the side. George idolized Mike, who taught him how
to ride and shoot. Mike also used George to help move
stolen cattle into Robber's Roost, a wild, barren plateau
in southeastern Utah that frequently served as both a
sanctuary and a base of operations for outlaws because
of its inaccessibility.

Young George learned his lessons well, becoming an
expert cattle rustler and horse thief while still in his
teens. To show his respect for Mike, George took the
last name of Cassidy. Before long, Mike found the law
getting too close for comfort, so he rode off for Mexico.
George went his own way soon after, finding work at
a mine in Colorado.

After a short stay he left the mine to join the Mc-Carty gang, and on November 3, 1887, George Cassidy attempted his first train robbery with the three Mc-Cartys—Bill, Tom, and George—and Matt Warner. The gang threatened to kill the express company messenger unless he opened the safe. When he stoutly refused, they backed down and took a vote on whether or not to rob the passengers. The vote was "no," and the gang rode off empty-handed into the Colorado countryside.

All was quiet for more than a year. Then, on March 30, 1889, Cassidy and Tom McCarty struck the First National Bank in Denver. Threatening the bank's president with a bottle of "nitroglycerin" (it was actually water), the two men fled with $21,000. Cassidy and the rest of the gang lay low in Star Valley, a bandit lair straddling the Wyoming-Idaho border. Although it was a long, hard ride from Denver, the area was safe and remote.

On June 24 the gang came out of hiding to hit another bank, this one in Telluride, in the southwestern part of Colorado. They got $10,500, then rode back to Star Valley and safety. The following spring the Mc-Cartys headed for Oregon, but Cassidy chose to stay behind. He drifted into Wyoming, where he worked as a cowhand for the next few years—and as a horse thief. On July 15, 1894, he was sent to prison. He was pardoned by Governor William A. Richards in January, 1896, after promising never again to cause trouble in the state. Otherwise unrepentant, Cassidy headed for the outlaw stronghold called Brown's Hole, tucked away in the southwestern corner of Wyoming, where the state touches Idaho and Utah.

Many outlaws gathered at Brown's Hole, among them Elza Lay (alias William McGuinness), Bob Meeks, and Cassidy's old friend from the McCarty gang, Matt Warner. From Matt, Cassidy learned that Bill and George McCarty had been killed during a bank robbery. Tom, the only McCarty to escape, had fled and disappeared from sight. Cassidy had by this time picked up the nickname "Butch"—a tag given to him while doing a stint as a butcher between 1890 and 1892. Butch, Lay, and the others became constant companions, and their drinking and carousing soon earned them the label of "the Wild Bunch."

On April 21, 1897, Butch and his Wild Bunch stole an $8,000 payroll from a mining camp at Castle Gate, Utah, about eighty-five miles southeast of Salt Lake City. News of the robbery, committed in broad daylight, reached the Logan brothers who, along with "Flat Nose" George Curry and many other outlaws, were in the mood to move from their Wyoming hideout in Hole in the Wall—the most famous outlaw retreat of all. Public pressure had been increasing for lawmen to "do something" about this hideout. Although attempts to invade the outlaw territory failed, the gunmen knew the end was near. In mid-1897 Harvey and Lonny Logan, Curry, and almost one hundred others left Hole in the Wall for the relative safety of Brown's Hole.

The outlaw gathering represented a small army of many of the toughest men in the country. Black Jack Ketchum and his brother Sam were there; Bill Carver, too; and Harry (the "Sundance Kid") Longbaugh and Harry Tracy.

Meanwhile, Cassidy, Elza Lay, and Bob Meeks robbed the Montpelier National Bank in Montpelier, Idaho, to get enough cash to hire a lawyer to defend Matt Warner, jailed earlier for a double murder. The robbery netted about $7,000, and Cassidy paid for the services of not one but four lawyers in an attempt to have his friend acquitted. Despite the lawyers and threats against witnesses, Warner was convicted and jailed for a five-year term. The outlaw trio returned to the Hole.

But more trouble was coming. Meeks had been identified as a member of the gang that robbed the Montpelier bank. Caught outside the protection of the Hole, he was arrested and eventually sentenced to a long stretch in prison. Three others from the lair soon found themselves in trouble when one of them, "Swede" Johnson, let his drinking get the best of him. Jostled by a sixteen-year-old boy while watching cowboys wrestling steers in the corral of a nearby ranch, the Swede shot and killed him. Forced to flee, Johnson met Harry Tracy and Dave Lant. The three decided to head for Colorado. A large posse, formed after the shooting, soon overtook the trio. In the gunfight that followed, Tracy gunned down Valentine Hoy, one of the brothers who owned the ranch where the murder occurred. The three outlaws were finally captured, but Tracy and Lant later escaped and split up. The Swede received a life sentence for the boy's murder, though he was subsequently freed on a reversed decision by a higher court.

The two killings only served to increase demands that the vast outlaw strongholds at Hole in the Wall, Brown's Hole, and others be broken up.

In the summer of 1897 a group of cattlemen, led by Robert Devine, decided to attack Hole in the Wall. Eleven heavily armed cattlemen rode into the outlaw country and fought a gun duel with three men from the Taylor gang. The result was two wounded cattlemen and one dead rustler. Devine returned with more men on August 10. They found no outlaws, but they recovered about 700 head of stolen cattle.

On June 2, 1899, Cassidy's gang, operating out of Brown's Hole, left their sanctuary for Wilcox, Wyoming. They had decided a train robbery would refill a depleted treasury. Cassidy planned the robbery, but perhaps because of his earlier promise to the Wyoming governor, he did not take a direct part. It was 2:30 a.m. when Curry, Lay, and Harvey Logan halted the Overland Flyer of the Union Pacific by waving a red lantern. Logan and Lay jumped into the cab and ordered the engineer to drive the train across a wooden bridge just ahead; Curry then dynamited the bridge. When the messenger refused to open up the express car, the outlaws blew the door in with explosives and made off with $60,000 in unsigned banknotes.

A posse set out in pursuit, picking up the trio's trail in Casper, where they had stopped to buy supplies. Tracked to Salt Creek, a rocky spot crisscrossed with gullies, the outlaws decided to make a fight of it. All night long the posse-men tried to reach the outlaws, but they were driven back. The next morning Logan got a clear shot at Sheriff Joe Hazen, fatally wounding him.

While the posse-men attended to the dying sheriff, the trio made a break for it. More men arrived to help in the manhunt, bringing the posse-men to several hundred. That night the outlaws decided on a bold scheme —they would turn back and sneak through the posse lines on foot. They made it without a scratch and then split up. Logan and Lay went South to join up with Cassidy and the gang, then in New Mexico Territory; Curry connected with a gang of horse thieves bound for Mexico.

The Wild Bunch, with Logan, Lay, and Blackjack and Sam Ketchum among them, pulled another raid on July 11, this time hitting a Colorado & Southern Railroad train near Folsom, New Mexico. The train's express messenger, however, outsmarted them. Ignoring the outlaws' threats to blow up the car, he opened the safe and hid its contents elsewhere, then relocked it as Cassidy's men smashed down the door. The safe was blown open, revealing nothing of value. The messenger explained that the money had been removed at the last stop and the gang rode off empty-handed.

They were tracked by a posse to the mountains near Cimarron. That night as the posse closed in on nearby Turkey Canyon to begin a careful search, gunfire suddenly erupted and a cowhand with the posse fell dead. Sheriff Farr, one of the leaders, was killed soon after. Four more men in the posse were wounded during the night; a deputy marshal was hit in the chest and died. The outlaws had their casualties. Sam Ketchum and Lay were wounded. The band decided to pull out, but Sam was too weak to ride. He asked to be left behind with his rifle. Lay and Logan managed to get away,

Butch Cassidy and the Wild Bunch. Standing: Bill Carver and Harvey Logan; seated: Harry Longbaugh, Ben Kilpatrick, and Butch Cassidy.

and later that night Sam made it to his horse and escaped. But he did not get far. The next day a rancher found him crumpled on the ground. Arrested and charged with murder, he died of blood poisoning in Santa Fe prison on July 24.

Logan rejoined Cassidy, but Lay, having fled to Carlsbad, New Mexico, to recover from his wounds, was captured, tried, and sentenced to life.

Curry left the gang and went into hiding in Utah. Tracked down by a posse in the spring of 1900, he was killed after a fierce fight. Blackjack Ketchum was captured next and died on the gallows.

Pressure increased on the remaining members of the gang—Cassidy, Harvey Logan (who out of respect for the dead George Curry, had taken the name Kid Curry for himself), Harry Longbaugh, "Deaf Charley" Hanks, Ben Kilpatrick (the "Tall Texan"), and his constant traveling companion Laura Bullion. Hiding places grew fewer as homesteaders flooded into the once-virgin country. Butch decided to pull out, to go to South America where everything was still wide open. To finance the move, the gang planned another train robbery.

The strike was just outside Tipton, Wyoming. Curry and Cassidy climbed into the engine cab, ordering the engineer to halt the train when he reached a small fire along the tracks. This was where Deaf Charley stood by with the getaway horses. Butch then forced the trainmen to uncouple the passenger cars from the engine, coal car, and the express car, which were moved down the track about a mile to give the men plenty of time to work on the express car. The express messenger turned out to be the same stubborn one the gang had come up against at Wilcox, and again, despite threats to blow him up, he refused to open the door. Finally, the conductor convinced the messenger that it was smarter to play along, and the door was opened. The gang set their dynamite charge after moving the messenger and conductor out of range. Unhappily, the charge was too big: it blew the safe to pieces, nearly demolished the car, and shredded the money into useless bits of paper. For all their trouble the gang recovered only $50 and some loose change. The total take rose by several hundred dollars, however, after they went back to the coaches and collected money from the passengers. Following the robbery the gang split up to shake off pursuit, agreeing to meet again several weeks later.

Although South America was still in their plans, the gang needed more money. They decided to hit a bank this time, but the question was where. Many of the areas once considered wide open were now too risky. They chose to keep riding: when they came upon a likely bank they would strike. In Nevada they were told of a bank at Winnemucca, which they promptly raided with success, escaping by horseback along a road that at one point paralleled the railroad line. Three different posses gave chase, one taking over an engine and flat car to catch the band by the railroad, but the outlaws slipped away.

In February, 1901, Butch, Longbaugh, and his mistress Etta Place made a trip to New York City. They stayed a few weeks shopping and looking at the big buildings like ordinary tourists. They had decided to go to South America, and this was to be the jumping off place. But before they could leave, Kid Curry wrote to Butch with plans for another robbery. Butch decided to take part, but Harry and Etta bought their steamship tickets for Buenos Aires. They agreed to meet Butch later.

The new strike was at Wagner, Montana, against the Great Northern Railroad, on July 3, 1901. The Wild Bunch, together for the last time, consisted of Cassidy, Kid Curry, Deaf Charley Hanks, the Tall Texan, and Laura Bullion. Curry boarded the train at Malta, and as the train got to Wagner he stepped into the engine. Pointing his two pistols at the engineer and fireman, he ordered the train stopped over a bridge where Butch, Ben, and Laura were waiting. Ben and Laura flanked the train and kept up a steady stream of bullets to prevent the passengers from causing trouble. Butch and Kid Curry shot open the lock on the express car, then placed a dynamite charge to blow the safe. This time they were more cautious and got the safe open without destroying its contents—$40,000 in bank notes. They joined Deaf Charley, who was in charge of the horses, and rode off. Though the bank notes lacked authorized signatures to make them valid, the gang took care of that problem by forging bank president and cashier names.

The Wild Bunch broke up: Butch to New York, then on to South America; Ben and Laura to St. Louis; Deaf Charley to Memphis; and Kid Curry, with his girlfriend, Annie, to Arkansas.

But the combination of luck and skill which had kept the Wild Bunch several steps ahead of the law was beginning to fade. Pinkerton detectives, never far behind, were now closing in. Curry and Annie narrowly escaped capture by moving only a few days before the Pinkertons arrived; Deaf Charley aroused suspicion in Nashville when he tried to cash one of the forged notes, and escaped under a hail of bullets; the Tall Texan cashed some bonds in St. Louis and was captured after a struggle with detectives. On December 12, 1901, he received a fifteen-year jail sentence. Laura was also taken after someone identified her as the outlaw's wife.

Kid Curry did not elude capture for long. On December 13, while shooting pool in Knoxville, he lost his temper when some bystanders joked about his playing. He beat up three of them, smashed the place to pieces, and shot two policemen who came in to see what was happening. He escaped, but twisted his ankle in the process. He was captured three days later.

Cassidy, Longbaugh, and Etta Place, now in Argentina, had established a homestead in Chubut Province, far from civilization. They settled down to a life of quiet ranching with a sizeable stock of cattle, sheep, and horses. But in March, 1903, a Pinkerton detective named Frank Dimaio received orders to shift from São Paulo, Brazil, to Buenos Aires, and to pick up the trio's trail. Inquiries soon turned up people who had seen them, including a dentist whose ranch was next to the one owned by the outlaws. It was the rainy season, however, and any attempt to penetrate the jungles surrounding Chubut was impossible. The detective instead had "Wanted" posters printed and widely distributed. He alerted everyone in the area; although it soon became known that the three Americans were on the run, little could be done about it. Their ranch, deep in tough country, lay on a high plateau and was virtually unassailable.

Three years passed quietly for the trio. Then, in 1906, perhaps because news of their identity and the offer of rewards for their capture began to circulate in their immediate area, the three left the ranch. When they next appeared it was at the Banco de la Nación in Villa Mercedes, Argentina. They had no difficulty in carrying out the robbery, returning briefly to their ranch to divide up the $20,000 in loot. This time a posse made it through the jungle to the hideout, but the gang had already left.

They split up to make detection more difficult, gathering again later in Santiago, Chile. They then returned to Argentina to hit the Banco de la Nación at Bahia Blanca. The take was again $20,000. Then on to Bolivia for an undisclosed amount of cash; then back to Argentina and a bank at Río Gallegos.

A short time later Etta got an attack of appendicitis, and she and the Sundance Kid returned to Denver, Colorado, to have it taken care of. She then vanished forever. The Sundance Kid returned to South America to join Butch, and in the summer of 1907 they went to work at the Concordia Tin Mines near La Paz, Bolivia.

They remained there for several months, then disappeared one day without even picking up their pay. Several days later, along with MacVey, another outlaw on the run, they robbed a Bolivian train, then melted into the jungle and headed for a hideout. MacVey, sane when sober, was an untrustworthy tiger when drunk—which was often—and before long Butch sent MacVey on his way and broke up the camp.

Butch and the Sundance Kid returned to the Concordia Tin Mines as suddenly as they had left, deciding to use the mine as a base of operations. Although the operators of the mine knew the real identities of the two men by now, they did nothing about it. There was no doubt that many of the mine's workers had something to hide—this was one reason why they worked there. The feeling was that so long as Butch and the Kid did not cause any trouble at the mine itself, what they did outside was their own business.

Train and bank robberies continued, and each time the two men struck they would dash back to the safety of the mine. During one robbery late in 1907 they got several thousand dollars from the Compañía Mercantil in Rio Gallegos, Argentina, but not before killing one man and wounding another when these two attempted to stop the robbery.

While Cassidy and Longbaugh operated with relative ease in South America, the end had come for others from the old Wild Bunch. Curry, serving a twenty-five-year term in the Federal prison at Columbus, Ohio, broke out after overpowering a guard and made his way to Colorado, where he got a job with a cow outfit. He soon went back to train robbing. On July 7, 1903, he and four others waylaid a train and blew open what proved to be an empty safe. A posse tracked them to an area near Glenwood Springs. Curry was mortally wounded in an all-night battle. He was found dead when the posse closed in during the early morning hours.

So now Harvey Logan, alias Kid Curry, was gone. Lonny Logan was dead, as was Blackjack Ketchum.

Carver was gunned down by a sheriff; Laura Bullion was in prison, along with Ben Kilpatrick, the Tall Texan; Flat-Nose George Curry was long gone.

Ben and Laura were eventually released from jail, but Ben was arrested while still in the warden's office for a murder in Texas. The two lovers spoke briefly together in the office before Ben was taken to Texas to stand trial. He was subsequently acquitted, but the two never met again.

On March 13, 1912, Ben and an outlaw named Howard Benson tried to rob the Southern Pacific Express near Sanderson, Texas. During the robbery, the express messenger killed the Tall Texan with one blow of a heavy ice mallet. Benson, searching the mail car, stepped into the express car to see what was happening and was killed by a shot from the messenger's rifle.

Elza Lay, one of the first of the Wild Bunch to be caught, was one of the few to survive. After his release from prison he moved to Wyoming, married, and passed the rest of his days in the relative quiet of the oil business.

Meanwhile, in Bolivia during the winter of 1912, Cassidy and the Sundance Kid robbed a mule train carrying the payroll of the Chocaya Tin-Silver Mine. There were only a few Indian guards, and the robbery was a breeze. But along with the money Butch took one of the mules—marked with the brand of the mine. Word spread quickly about the payroll robbery, and Cassidy and Longbaugh now found that the people who had befriended, or at least tolerated them, had now had enough. He and Longbaugh were forced to

One of the many posses that trailed the Wild Bunch.

move, eventually making their way to San Vicente, thirty-five miles from the site of the robbery. This time they were tracked by police and soldiers, who arrived in San Vicente only hours after the outlaws reached there. They found the branded mule and the bandits in

a *barrio*, or corral, surrounded by a ten-foot wall. Butch and the Kid were inside a small hut, their rifles leaning against the wall outside. Called on to surrender, the outlaws replied with bullets, killing one of the soldiers. The posse returned the fire, keeping it up until all was quiet in the hut. No one attempted to enter the hut until ten o'clock the following morning. Butch Cassidy and the Sundance Kid were both dead.

RUBE
BURROWS

REUBEN HOUSTON BURROWS WAS BORN IN LAMAR County, Alabama, on December 11, 1854. He was one of ten children born to Allen H. Burrows and Martha Caroline Terry, who had married in 1849. Rube's brother Jim, the fifth and youngest son, was born in 1858. His father taught in a small country school although he had little formal education himself. During the Civil War Mr. Burrows served with the Confederate cavalry, but on his return to civilian life his interest turned from teaching to moonshining. In 1876 he went into hiding to avoid arrest for illicit distilling, coming back home two years later to quietly live out the rest of his life.

As a boy Rube loved the freedom of the outdoor life. He was described as an "active, sprightly boy, apt in all athletic pursuits, a swift runner, and an ardent huntsman and natural woodsman." Rube left his home for Texas in 1872. Like many emigrants from the South, he had heard the tales of great fortunes and opportunities to be found in Texas. He was eighteen years old when he arrived to live on his uncle Joel Burrows' small farm in Erath County. His brother Jim joined him in 1876, the year Mr. Burrows disappeared from the family home in Lamar County. Jim remained in Texas until 1880, when he returned to Alabama to marry. In 1884 he rejoined Rube in Texas, bringing his wife along. His two trips to Texas coincided with Rube's marriages: in 1876, Rube married Virginia Alvison in Wise County, who bore him two children before she died of unreported causes in 1880; Rube remarried in 1884, this time to Adeline Hoover of Erath County.

The two brothers drifted around the state working as cowboys, but the cattle industry was by then in decline and work was scarce. Rube's skill as a horseman and a marksman, however, drew men to him, and by 1886 he was the acknowledged head of a four-man band that grew increasingly restless over the lack of money and excitement. On December 1, 1886, they decided to try a change of luck.

Rube, Jim, Nep Thornton, and Henderson Bromley rode to the Bellevue station of the Fort Worth and Denver Railway. They hid their horses in the woods nearby and crept up on a water tank about three hundred yards from the station. At eleven o'clock that morning the train stopped at the tank to take on water. Thornton held the engineer and fireman prisoner while Rube, Jim, and Bromley walked through the coaches robbing the passengers. Also on the train was a squad of soldiers in charge of some prisoners. Rube promptly relieved the soldiers of their forty-five caliber, single-action pistols, two of which were to remain with him for the rest of his life. He then ordered the prisoners set free. The prisoners looked the outlaws over, glanced at their captors, and chose to stay with the guards. Rube signaled his party to make for their horses. Besides the soldiers' guns the outlaws had $300 and more than a dozen watches from the passengers for their trouble.

The following January they planned another raid. The gang met at Alexander, Texas, then rode seventy-five miles to Gordon, Texas, a station on the Texas and Pacific Railway. They reached there soon after midnight on January 23, 1887. As the train pulled slowly out of Gordon at two o'clock, Rube and Bromley swung aboard the engine and ordered the engineer and fireman to bring the train to a halt five hundred yards down the track. When the train stopped, Jim, Thornton, and Harrison Askew, a new recruit, were waiting. But as the men prepared to climb abroad, Askew lost his nerve: he dashed to his horse and rode off. The other outlaws got down to business. Rube and Bromley escorted the engineer and fireman to the express car while Jim and Thornton held their guns on the conductor and the trainman.

The Pacific Express Company messenger at first refused Rube's demand that he open up and put out the lights in the car as if preparing for a fight. The outlaws leveled their Winchesters at the door and fired more than fifty bullets into the door before the messenger surrendered. The haul was about $2,275 in cash from the express car safe, and $2,000 from registered mail in an adjoining mail car.

Soon after the robbery the gang split up to avoid suspicion. Thornton took this opportunity to quit the gang and was not heard from again. The Burrowses and their families settled together on a ranch in Erath County, located in the central part of Texas, hiring an illiterate but strong young man named William Brock to help with the chores. Brock soon became a close friend and a member of the gang.

In the spring of 1887, Rube decided to make another strike at Gordon, and sent word to Bromley to come to the Burrows farm near Stephensville. On May 10 the gang rode for the Brazos River, some fifty miles away. When they arrived the river was overflowing its banks because of spring rains; it was impossible to cross. They rescheduled the robbery for the following month.

On June 3 the gang met again at the Burrows farm. Having learned of a better target for the robbery, they planned to hit the Ben Brook station, seventy-five miles south of Fort Worth, of the Texas and Pacific. The next day the four men rode to Ben Brook, where a long railroad trestle crossed a steep gorge. At seven o'clock that night Rube and Bromley, their faces blackened with cork, boarded the train and ordered the engineer to halt the train on the trestle, leaving the engine on solid ground. This technique isolated the passengers and kept them from causing trouble. Jim and Brock then came aboard, smashed open the express car door with a coal pick, and scooped up $2,450. The gang made an easy escape under cover of a heavy rain.

109

Three months later, on September 2, 1887, the gang struck again—robbing the same train at the same spot, and getting nearly the same amount of money, $2,725.

The Burrowses, along with Jim's wife and Rube's two children, left Texas in mid-November for a visit to their parents' home in Vernon, Alabama. They started back to Texas in December, but near the Red River Rube and Jim spotted a likely holdup spot— Genoa, Arkansas—thirty miles north of Texarkana. Brock was hastily summoned and the details of the robbery worked out. On the night of December 9, two of the outlaws boarded the engine of Express Train No. 2 of the St. Louis, Arkansas and Texas Railway, as it left Genoa. The engineer and fireman were ordered to stop the train about one and a half miles down the track, where the third member of the gang waited. As the train pulled to a halt the outlaw stepped forward and started firing his rifle at the coaches to keep the passengers down in their seats. The other two outlaws went to the express car and ordered the messenger to open the door. When he refused they forced the engineer to spread oil around the car. Under the threat of being burned alive, the messenger opened the door. The gang rode away with about $2,000 in cash.

A posse was soon on its way from Texarkana, where the outlaws were headed. Deciding to bluff their way out of possible capture, they tied their horses to some trees in a gully and then nonchalantly strolled into town. A few miles outside of Texarkana the posse came on the three men walking along the railroad track. It was about three o'clock in the morning and the trio passed by, seemingly safe. Suddenly, the posse turned and ordered the men to halt. The outlaws broke for cover and began shooting. Soon the firing stopped, but the posse decided to hold its ground until daylight, discovering then that the outlaws had slipped safely away.

Unfortunately, important pieces of evidence had been left behind: two rubber raincoats and a slouch hat. The coats were eventually traced to a store in Alexander, Texas, where the clerk recalled selling one to a man named Brock, who lived nearby in Dublin. On December 31, Brock was captured at his farm. He talked freely, implicating the Burrowses in the holdup. He told detectives that following the gunfight near Texarkana he had headed for Texas, while Rube and Jim made for Lamar County, Alabama.

On January 5, 1888, three Pinkerton men left Texarkana for Lamar County, where they were joined by the county sheriff on January 8. They headed for Jim Burrows' home at Vernon, but the outlaw spotted them in time to slip away. Friends and relatives of the brothers immediately sent word to Rube, who was in hiding at Kennedy, Alabama, eighteen miles away. And on January 10 the two men secretly met and left the area. Two weeks later, as they boarded a southbound Louisville and Nashville train headed for Montgomery, they were recognized by a conductor who had seen one of the "Wanted" circulars distributed by the Southern Express Company. He wired ahead so that when the train pulled into the station at Montgomery detec-

111

$7,500 REWARD

Murderers and Train Robbers.

The Southbound Express train on the Mobile & Ohio Railway was robbed on the morning of Sept. 25, 1889, by three masked men, who are the same parties who robbed the Illinois Central train on Dec. 15, 1888, and murdered Chester Hughes, a passenger, in so doing.

No. 1.—Reuben Houston Burrow, alias Charles Davis, is described as follows: About 34 years old, 6 feet 1 inch tall, weight about 170 lbs., light complexion, dark sandy hair, long drooping mustache, possibly chin and side whiskers of recent growth, inclined to be sandy. The eyes are blue, small and deep-set, giving the brow a protruding appearance; nose short and appears stubby. Teeth sound and upper front teeth project slightly outward. Lower jaws prominent and protrude noticeably backward under ears. Hair on top of head very thin. Head round. When spoken to generally throws head backward displaying Adams apple in replying to questions. Speaks abruptly and rather quickly. Right arm little shorter than left arm. Wears 7¼ hat and 7½ boot. He neither smokes nor chews. Has a habit of telling funny stories and also of quoting and ridiculing the Bible. Has small scar scarcely noticeable on forehead over left eyebrow, made by bird shot. Has a small mole on the right cheek bone. When last seen wore dark colored coat, gray jeans pants, and reddish brown slouch hat, with narrow leather band and leather binding, known as a cowboy's hat. Is very restless and always watchful.

No. 2.—Joe Jackson, alias Henry Davis. About 30 years old; 5 feet 8 inches high; weight about 165 lbs. to 170 lbs.; black hair, black whiskers and mustache, whiskers generally worn full but are thin on side of face. Dark complexion; eyes, black and round. Has noticeable scar on left side of cheek or neck, also scar high up on forehead, which he keeps concealed by wearing his hair hanged over it. Manner reticent and avoids looking at one when talking. Frequently complains of rheumatism in lower limbs, and occasionally, especially in wet weather, limps, but the limping is caused by gunshot wounds and not from rheumatism. His body and limbs are covered with gunshot wounds. He is compactly built and has round face. When last seen, wore dark rough suit, with cutaway coat and dark slouch hat.

No. 3.—About 30 years old; weight, 145 lbs.; 5 feet 9 inches high; rather slim in build; black hair and black eyes; black mustache and whiskers, of recent growth; dark complexion, face rather long. When last seen, wore dark mixed clothing and black slouch hat.

These men are all coarsely dressed, and might be taken for farmers or country laborers. They carried two small satchels and rubber overcoats, and one or more Winchester rifles; also small bundle. All wore heavy pistols and leather belts with cartridges. Numbers one and two are generally found in company with each other, and pass as brothers, though they do not personally resemble each other.

The following rewards are offered for the arrest and delivery of the men who committed the robberies above named, and for their delivery to any one of the undersigned:

By the Mobile and Ohio Railroad and Southern Express Company, $2000.00.

By the United States Government, $1000.00 each.

By the Illinois Central Railroad Company and the Southern Express Company, $1000.00.

By the State of Mississippi, $500.00.

By the State of Arkansas and the St. Louis, Arkansas & Texas Railway Company, $500.00.

By the State of Alabama, $500.00.

Total reward, $7,500.00.

Wire or write information to D. McLaren, Supt., Mobile & Ohio Railway, Mobile, Ala.; G. W. Agee, Supt., Southern Express Company, Memphis, Tenn.; A. G. Sharp, Postoffice Inspector, Chattanooga, Tenn.; J. G. Mann, Supt., Illinois Central Railroad, New Orleans, La.; H. C. Fisher, Supt., Southern Express Company, Nashville, Tenn., or the Governors of the above named States.

The outlaws were recognized by a conductor who had seen one of the "Wanted" circulars.

112

tives were waiting. As Rube and Jim stepped off the train and started to walk away, two men, dressed in rubber raincoats and slouch hats, came up and asked where they were headed. Not suspecting a trap, the outlaws replied that they were looking for a hotel. The disguised lawmen suggested some places and offered to show the way. The four men strolled along until they reached the front of a darkened building. As one of the lawmen started to unlock the door, he calmly announced that this was the jail and the brothers were under arrest.

Rube and Jim made a break for it. Jim was overpowered, but Rube got away. A group of citizens formed a posse and raced after him. To their surprise, Rube had stopped running and had set up an ambush. In the gunfight that followed one posse man was severely wounded. Rube slipped off. The next day he was tracked to a cabin near Montgomery, but again he eluded capture.

Rube made his way back into Lamar County in February, determined to find a way to free Jim. Unsuccessful in an attempt to get in touch with Frank Jackson from the old Sam Bass gang, Rube then asked Lewis Waldrip, a notorious gunman whom he had met while in Texas in 1886, to join them. The two men watched for an opportunity to free Jim, but he died in Little Rock Penitentiary on October 5 after a week of delirium due to a fever.

On December 15, Rube and Waldrip struck an Illinois Central Railway train as it pulled out of the Duck Hill, Mississippi, station shortly after ten o'clock at night. As the outlaws climbed into the car, the engineer mistook them for tramps because of their rough clothes. He started to slow the engine to put them off when he noticed he was covered by their pistols. The outlaws ordered the train stopped and then forced the engineer and fireman ahead of them to the express car. The express messenger opened the door on command, but at that moment a conductor stepped off one of the coaches to see why the train had stopped. He was ordered back in the coach, but once inside he passed the alarm and asked for help. Chester Hughes, a young boy from Jackson, Tennessee, volunteered. Hughes and the conductor obtained rifles, stepped off the train into the darkness, and started shooting.

At the first shot the engineer dashed to the safety of the nearby woods. The gunfight was over within minutes. Neither Rube nor Waldrip was hit, but Hughes lay mortally wounded with three bullets in his stomach. The outlaws escaped after a half-mile walk to where their horses were hidden. They returned to Lamar County with about $2,000 from the holdup.

On June 1 of the following year, Rube wrote away for a light-red, short-cropped wig from Chicago, giving the fictitious name of W. W. Cain and a return address in Sulligent, Alabama. His handwriting, however, was illegible, and the package was forwarded to the post office in nearby Jewell. When the package arrived it was split open enough for its contents to be seen by Moses Graves, the postmaster. Suspicious, Graves decided to turn the claimant over to the police. Rube took the precaution of sending Jim Cash, his brother-in-law, to claim the package. But the ruse failed: the post-master stubbornly refused to turn it over to anyone but Cain.

On June 7, Rube came down to the post office after it had been closed for the night and pounded on the door, demanding the package. Graves would not open up. In a fury, Rube smashed the window and shot Graves as his terrified wife looked on.

The postmaster soon died, but not before he identified Burrows as his assailant. A posse quickly formed, but once again the outlaw escaped without a trace. He and Waldrip remained out of sight until the fall.

On September 26 the outlaws rode for Buckatunna, Mississippi, to hit the Mobile & Ohio. They were accompanied by Rube Smith, an escaped robber and a first cousin of Rube Burrows.

At two-thirty o'clock the following morning Rube and Waldrip stepped into the engine cab of the southbound express at the Buckatunna station. They ordered the train moved down the tracks several hundred yards to the trestle over Buckatunna Creek, so that the passengers could not get off. The engineer stopped the train at the spot where Smith was waiting beside the tracks. The conductor stepped off the train to see what was causing the delay, but he bounded back aboard when a bullet whistled over his head. The outlaw trio then proceeded to the express car, where they got $2,685. The mail car yielded $795.

When the holdup was over, Rube ordered the engineer and fireman to get steam up in the engine and move on. "Don't ring the bell or blow the whistle," Rube ordered, "or I will shoot into the engine." As a parting gesture, Rube confided to the engineer that he had robbed the train simply because there had been a boast in the newspapers the previous spring that it could not be done. The outlaws then faded into the brush as the train picked up speed. The Mobile & Ohio train dispatcher's log for that day explained: "Number five delayed thirty minutes at Buckatunna trestle, getting robbed."

Rube Smith left Burrows and Waldrip near Demopolis, Alabama, about October 5, to continue the journey alone. Rube and Waldrip made their way back to Lamar County, reaching there on October 23. By mid-December it had become too risky for them to stay together: both Pinkerton men and detectives for the Southern Express Company were on their trail. The two outlaws separated at Flomaton, Alabama, on December 14, agreeing to meet again in Baldwin County on February 20, 1890, in order to rob the Louisville & Nashville train at Dyer's Creek, some thirty miles north of Mobile.

On the same day that Rube and Waldrip split up, Smith was arrested in Amory, Alabama, after attracting the attention of the police by flashing around his share of the Buckatunna robbery. He was later convicted of the robbery and sentenced to ten years in prison.

In February, Waldrip left Lamar County for his prearranged meeting with Rube. When Rube failed to appear, Waldrip headed back. Unknown to him, detectives had learned of his presence and had staked out Allen Burrows' house on the theory that Waldrip would eventually pay him a visit. It was a long wait, but the vigil paid off. On July 15, Jim Cash and Waldrip were seen leaving the house and heading for the Georgia Pacific Railroad station at Fernbank. About five miles from the station, Cash turned back. Detectives of the Southern Express Company followed Waldrip as he boarded the train, one of them, Tom Jackson, taking a seat immediately behind the outlaw. No attempt was made to arrest Waldrip on the train because of the possible risk to other passengers, but as he stepped off the train at Columbus, Mississippi, detectives waited with drawn guns. Waldrip, whose real name was Leonard Calvert Brock, was captured without a struggle.

Rube had headed for Florida after leaving Waldrip at Flomaton. He crossed into Florida on December 15, unaware that he was being tracked every step of the way by Tom Jackson. Jackson crossed the Escambia River at McCurdy's ferry on January 29, about forty-five days behind Burrows. By persistent and thorough questioning of people along the way, Jackson kept on Rube's trail. At Broxton's ferry on the Yellow River, thirty miles south of the Escambia River crossing point, the detective's luck improved. He learned from another man that Rube was working in that very area hauling feed from the landing opposite the ferry to a logging camp eighteen miles away. He was jubilant at the prospect of finally capturing Rube. To his superiors at the express company he telegraphed: "I expect to secure title to tract number one, about ten miles south of here, Wednesday, February 6th. The papers are all in good shape." Tract number one was, of course, Rube Burrows.

On the morning of February 6, Jackson, joined by four other men from the express company, lay in hiding for Rube to walk into the trap. They knew that this was the day scheduled for Rube to return to the ferry landing for another load of supplies. Every other day for five straight weeks Rube had come to the landing between two and three o'clock in the afternoon. The posse waited in vain. At five o'clock a laborer from the camp appeared. He told the detectives that one of Ward's (Rube's alias) oxen was sick, delaying the trip. The posse decided to wait, but by seven o'clock they concluded that the outlaw would not come until the following day. They moved down the road to an empty house, where they intended to remain overnight. As they reached the house—about a mile from the ferry— Rube arrived at the landing. He asked Mrs. Broxton about her husband, and when she told him that her husband had been with a party of hunters all day, Rube suspected trouble. He cautiously investigated, spotting the posse without being seen himself. He immediately raced back to the logging camp, gathered some provisions, and disappeared into the Santa Rosa swamps in the northwestern part of Florida.

Undaunted by Rube's escape, Jackson took up the trail again. On February 15, he reached another landing on the Yellow River to learn that Rube had crossed by ferry only an hour before. As the boat had not yet returned, Jackson plunged into the swift water and swam to the other shore. He then made his way along the river bank until he met the boy who had taken Rube across. He found that the outlaw's lead was now only thirty minutes. Jackson raced ahead in the desperate hope of overtaking Rube. Darkness came before he could catch sight of the outlaw, and Jackson was forced to make camp for the night. When dawn came, the detective found that the trail was lost. He headed back for Lamar County.

Rube made his way to the vicinity of East Bay, a rugged area of swamp and jungle about four miles from the Gulf Coast. Here he stayed with Charles Wells and his family throughout the spring and summer of 1890. Wells, who had a reputation for offering refuge to men on the run, lived in a dilapidated cabin amid the canebrakes. The area was relatively uninhabited and nearly inaccessible. Rube had good reason to feel safe from capture.

Nevertheless, Rube came out of hiding on September 1, climbing into the cab of the Louisville & Nashville train at Flomaton, Alabama, seventy-five miles from his camp in the swamp. On command, the engineer stopped the train on the north side of the Escambia River Bridge, only the engine and express car on solid ground. Armed with two forty-five caliber pistols, Rube forced the engineer and fireman out of the cab. As soon as the fireman reached the ground he broke away and dashed into the woods. Rube ordered the engineer to smash down the express car door with a coal pick taken from the coal tender. When the door was opened, the messenger inside stood gun in hand. Rube threatened to kill the engineer unless the messenger dropped his gun. This done, Rube handed the engineer a sack to hold while the messenger emptied into it the contents of the safe, only $256.19, plus his pistol. Rube then disappeared into the wood, eventually making his way back into the swamps.

Detectives suspected that Rube would head for the Wells cabin. They marched on the site, led by John Barnes, who had known Rube from the lumber camp. When the posse reached the cabin there was no sign of the outlaw, although some of his clothes and money were found. The detectives took the Wells family into custody and placed a guard at the house. Other members of the posse spread out through the swamps. Rube fled the area and crossed into Alabama on September 25. He appeared at the Barnes home, just across the Florida-Alabama line, four days later, asking for breakfast and supplies. While Barnes, unsuspected as an informer, kept Rube busy with conversation, his wife slipped away and sent word to detectives.

The detectives, thinking that Rube would probably head for his home town, set out to intercept him at Bell's Landing, a spot some fifty miles from the Barnes place and on the route to Lamar County. They guarded the landing all night, but learned the next morning that Rube was having breakfast in a sharecropper's home six miles away. They rode to the cabin, but again too late—thirty minutes earlier Rube had rowed across the Alabama River in the only available boat, forcing the posse to detour six miles to the south to get across.

When the posse reached Thomasville, Alabama, on October 4, they found that Rube had passed through there only two hours before.

On October 7, a man named Jesse Hildreth found

Rube sound asleep in an abandoned cabin. He woke the outlaw before realizing who he was. Keeping his wits, Hildreth acted as though he believed Rube to be just a poor traveler. He offered to sell him a horse, but Rube replied that he only wanted to be shown the way to Blue Lick. Hildreth offered to show him the way. They went on until noon, when it began to rain. Hildreth suggested that they go to the nearby cabin of a friend, George Ford. During dinner, Rube got up to look around outside. Hildreth managed to pass the word to a fellow named Frank Marshall that Burrows was with him. Marshall promptly alerted the posse.

The detectives decided that Marshall should return to the cabin and rejoin Hildreth. Because of their physical strength and size, the two men were given the responsibility of overpowering Burrows. Once this was done, they were to signal the detectives to close in.

The two men entered the cabin, waited until Rube was off his guard, then jumped him. The outlaw fought like a wild man. The battle inside the cabin caused such a racket that the detectives decided not to wait for the signal. They broke in and made the capture certain.

Rube was taken to the county jail at Linden on October 7. There, while having supper, his handcuffs were removed. The leg irons were kept on. Several guards were assigned to watch him: Jim McDuffie, Frank Marshall, and Jesse Hildreth. The evening and most of the night passed quietly. Near dawn on October 8, Rube woke up and told McDuffie that he was hungry. He asked for his ration bag. After McDuffie handed it

121

*A grisly portrait
of the late Rube
Burrows, by
an unidentified
photographer.*

over, Rube sat and ate some ginger snaps and candy. He reached into his bag once more, this time withdrawing his forty-five. He ordered the leg irons removed, then proceeded to handcuff McDuffie and Marshall together. He insisted that Hildreth help him and J. D. Carter, one of the posse-men, who was holding his money and rifle.

Carter was asleep in a nearby store. Hildreth knocked on the door and asked Carter to step outside. When he appeared, Rube jammed a pistol to his chest and demanded his money and his rifle. Carter reached into his hip pocket, but instead of money he pulled out a thirty-two caliber pistol. Rube jumped back and fired, hitting Carter in the shoulder, just above the collar bone. But as the wounded man sagged in pain, he got off four shots. Rube retreated, emptying his gun at Carter. The outlaw then turned to run. As Carter dropped to his knees he fired a fifth time. Rube ran about ten steps, seemed to jump into the air, and fell dead. Later examination showed that of the five shots fired by Carter, only the fourth hit its target. Rube's last five shots all went wild.

THE
DALTONS
vs
COFFEYVILLE

THE DALTONS HAD BEEN YOUNGSTERS WHEN JESSE James and the Youngers were in their prime and, in fact, lived about a half-day's ride from the bandits' homesteads. Bob Dalton had often heard the stories about the daring Northfield, Minnesota, raid. He dreamed of some day pulling a job that would overshadow Jesse's adventure.

When the Daltons rode into Coffeyville, Kansas, on October 5, 1892, they had behind them a string of four train robberies, only the first of which had been unsuccessful. In February of 1891 they had attempted to rob the Atlantic Express of the Southern Pacific at Alila, in Tulare County, California. During the holdup George Radliff, the fireman, was shot and killed. The outlaws failed to open the safe because the express messenger, who knew the combination to the lock, had fled. So did the gang—empty-handed.

In May they held up a Santa Fe train at Wharton, in the Cherokee Strip, getting about $14,000; in June of the following year they struck at Red Rock, in the Oklahoma Territory, getting only $2,000; and, on July 14, they robbed the Missouri, Kansas & Texas at Adair, in Oklahoma Territory, escaping with approximately $17,000 after a gun battle that resulted in the killing of one person and the wounding of several others.

Flushed with success, Bob Dalton told the others in the gang about the next job—a double bank robbery in broad daylight in Coffeyville, where the Daltons were well known.

Coffeyville lay along the Verdigris River on the southern border of Montgomery County, Kansas, about one-and-a-half miles from the northern boundary of the Indian Territory. The gang—Gratton, Bob, and Emmet Dalton, Bill Powers, Dick Broadwell, and Bill Doolin—headed for Coffeyville from a rendezvous point north of Tulsa in the Osage Nation, about thirty miles away. On the way, Doolin's horse went lame, and he turned back to get a fresh one; before he could catch up the raid was over.

The night before the attack the riders pulled up and made camp on Onion Creek, at the farm of P. L. Davis, some three miles out of Coffeyville. Bob drew a map of the town in the dust and described the route the gang would take going in and out. Of the two banks in the town—the First National and the C. M. Condon & Company Bank, a private institution—the First National was farthest from where their horses would be tied; it was considered the tougher assignment. A coin was flipped for it—Emmet and Bob calling heads, the others tails. It came up heads. Before they went to sleep the men burned all their personal papers to confuse identification in case any of the men were captured.

Plans for the escape were worked out: ride to the Cherokee Strip where a wagon would be waiting with supplies and ammunition; then to No Man's Land disguised as emigrants; finally, into the mountains of New Mexico.

After a breakfast of biscuits, hard-boiled eggs, and coffee, they broke camp, timing their ride to reach the town just after nine o'clock, when it would be quiet. This was important, since they were known to many of the employees of the two banks, the shop keepers, and "every law officer in town."

The day of the Dalton's first daylight holdup and first bank robbery began auspiciously. It was clear and cool. Numerous people saw the riders but there was no reason to be suspicious. One man said later that he thought the party was a deputy U.S. marshal with his posse. The Daltons rode into town on Eighth Street until they reached Maple, but, discovering that the chosen hitching spot for their horses had been torn down, they moved on and settled for the fence at the rear of an empty lot belonging to Police Judge Munn. After hitching their horses, they walked along an alley that opened up on the town's central plaza. They passed a stone-cutter on the way, who noticed they were armed but thought nothing more of it.

Straight ahead was the First National Bank, one of

$5,000 REWARD

Bob, Emmet, Grat

DALTON

The Dalton brothers were known to every law officer in Coffeyville.

a number of buildings on the east side of the plaza. The bank was flanked on the south by Isham Bros. & Mansur's hardware store. On the north side of the plaza was the Condon Bank. Grat, Powers, and Broadwell went into the bank; Bob and Emmet quickly crossed the street and headed for the First National.

Before the trio reached the Condon Bank, however, they passed a man named Charlie Gump. He noticed something odd: the men had on false beards, and one of them looked familiar. Curious, Gump watched as the three men entered the bank. From his vantage point atop a wagon he could see through the bank's front window. He was startled to see one of the men pointing a Winchester toward the cashier's counter.

Gump sounded the alarm; it was picked up and repeated across the plaza.

There were three employees inside the Condon Bank when Grat, Powers, and Broadwell entered: C. T. Carpenter, a bank officer; T. C. Babb, a bookkeeper; and C. M. Ball, the cashier. Grat handed Ball a grain sack to hold open, and ordered Carpenter to empty into it the money from the counter and the cash drawer. The outlaws also grabbed three bags of silver worth $3,000.

Grat demanded that the safe be opened. Ball hesitated before replying, "It is not time for that to open." He told Grat that it was only 9:20; the time-lock would not open until 9:30. (The fact that it was then really 9:30 was beside the point: the safe had been open since 8:00). The trick worked. Grat decided to wait ten minutes for the safe to open. Inside lay $18,000.

Two customers entered the bank and were made prisoners. Suddenly, gunfire erupted from outside and bullets smashed through the windows of the bank. The citizens, alerted by Gump's alarm, had armed themselves and taken up positions around the plaza.

Meanwhile, Emmet and Bob had entered the First National Bank, scooping up the money from the counter, in addition to gold and currency from the vault. Inside the bank were Thomas G. Ayres, the cashier,

W. H. Shepard, the teller, and B. S. Ayres, the book-keeper. There were also four customers, one of whom had followed the outlaws into the bank thinking that they, too, were depositors.

Bob Dalton ordered the bankers to march out the front door ahead of Emmet and himself. As they reached the sidewalk two shots were fired from Rammel Bros. drugstore adjoining the bank on the north. The party retreated into the bank. Bob stepped to the door and returned the fire, then ordered the employees and customers out a rear door to get them out of the way.

The town's hardware stores, where guns and ammunition were for sale, became supply depots for all comers. Weapons were loaded and handed out to the citizens, who proceeded to blast away at the banks.

The first man to be hit was Gump. After giving the alarm he had gone into Isham's to get a shotgun, and when he stepped back outside Bob Dalton, firing from the doorway of the bank, dropped him.

The first to die was Lucius Baldwin, a clerk. He, too, got a gun from Isham's, but instead of going out the front door he went the back way, into the alley that ran behind the whole row of stores and the First National Bank. As Baldwin stepped into the alley so did Bob and Emmet. "Hold up there!" Bob shouted, but Baldwin either did not hear him or, perhaps, thought they were fellow citizens. He came toward them until Bob pulled the trigger of his Winchester.

The two outlaws ran down the alley to the corner, where it met Eighth Street. They turned west up Eighth to Union, the street fronting the stores and emptying into the plaza. They got to the middle of Union when they spotted George Cubine, another armed citizen, standing in the doorway of the Rammel Bros. drug store. Bob Dalton fired again, and Cubine dropped, mortally wounded. Charles Brown ran to the dying man and picked up his rifle. Bob fired and Brown fell; he died three hours later.

Tom Ayres, the First National's cashier who had been turned out of the bank by the Daltons, also picked up a gun from Isham's. He took up a position in front of the store where he commanded a view of the bank. He had not reckoned with Bob Dalton's marksmanship. The two outlaws, heading for their horses, were nearly seventy-five yards away. Bob turned, aimed, and brought Ayres down with one shot.

Bob and Emmet went up Eighth Street and into an alley running behind a group of stores facing the plaza from the west, and for a few minutes they were out of sight. At the same time, Grat, Powers, and Broadwell emerged from the Condon Bank, backing slowly across the wide plaza toward the alley down which they had come. At the other end of this alley, near Maple Street, their horses—and escape—waited. Bob and Emmet had by now come out from behind the stores and stood at the junction of the two alleys.

At the first sound of alarm Henry Isham, one of the owners of the hardware store, armed with a Winchester, had stationed himself and three other men—Lewis Deitz, N. M. Anderson and Charles Smith—at a point facing the entire plaza, including the alley directly across from the First National Bank. As the out-

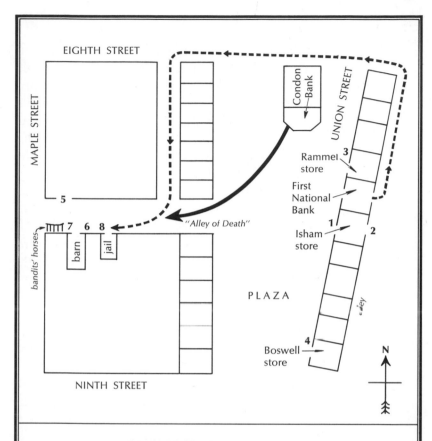

EIGHTH STREET

MAPLE STREET

UNION STREET

Condon Bank

Rammel store

First National Bank

Isham store

"Alley of Death"

 bandits' horses

7 6 8

barn jail

5

3

1 2

PLAZA

4

Boswell store

N

NINTH STREET

BANK ROBBERY AT COFFEYVILLE

1	Gump and Ayres wounded.	5	Powers killed.
2	Baldwin killed.	6	Connelly killed.
3	Cubine and Brown killed.	7	Grat killed.
4	Isham party's position.	8	Bob killed and Emmet wounded.

------► Route followed by Bob and Emmet.

────► Retreat of Grat, Powers, and Broadwell.

law trio came out of the Condon Bank, Isham and his party opened fire. The five outlaws, now together, started up the long alley toward their mounts. Grat and Powers were hit before they could reach the horses. The wounded Powers tried to duck into a doorway, but it was locked. He went on and managed to reach his horse. But as he started to mount, a bullet caught him in the back and he fell dead.

Grat ducked behind an oil tank and made his way to the side of a barn where, shielded by a stairway, he was out of the line of fire from the hardware store. He stayed here, occasionally returning the citizens' fire. Then the city marshal, C. T. Connelly, stepped into the alley Bob and Emmet had come through not long before. Unwittingly, Connelly exposed himself long enough for Grat to pull the trigger. Grat then tried to make it to his horse, but John Kloehr killed him with a bullet in the throat. The marshal died of his wound near the end of the battle.

Broadwell had also been wounded but he managed to reach cover. He rested until there was a lull in the shooting, then made his break. He reached his horse and dashed for safety. After riding no more than twenty feet, he was hit by both rifle and shotgun fire. Bleeding severely, he hung on as his horse took him back out of the town by the same route he had come only twenty minutes earlier. He was later found dead about a half-mile out of town, lying by the road.

As Bob and Emmet moved down the "alley of death" toward the horses they spotted a man climbing out through the rear window of a store. He ducked back inside as Bob fired, missing him. Bob then stepped out into the center of the alley and looked up at the roof-tops, perhaps in the belief that he could pick off any-one shooting from there. Instead, the men in Isham's store got him in their sights and fired, wounding him badly. He staggered across the alley and sat down on a pile of curbstones, continuing to fire. But he was weak and his aim was bad. He stood up and made it to the side of a barn west of the jail, but he was still short of where the horses were tied. Leaning against the corner of the building for support, he managed to get off sev-eral more shots before Kloehr put a bullet in his chest.

So far Emmet had not been hit. He kept out of sight until it was time to mount up. As he did, rifle bullets hit him in the right arm, hip, and groin. He pulled him-self into the saddle, clinging tightly to the money sack from the First National.

Then, instead of making a run for it, he rode to where his brother Bob lay. He leaned over and held out his hand. Bob could only say, "It's no use" before Emmet took both barrels of a shotgun in his back. He tumbled off his horse, the $20,000 still with him. Bob died within a few moments. Emmet was surrounded and taken prisoner. David Elliott described the holo-caust in *Last Raid of the Daltons*, a little blue-covered paperback book published on October 22, 1892:

> *The scene that was presented in the "alley of death" was ghastly beyond human conception. A moment or two passed after the cry went up, "They are all down!" before anyone ventured to*

133

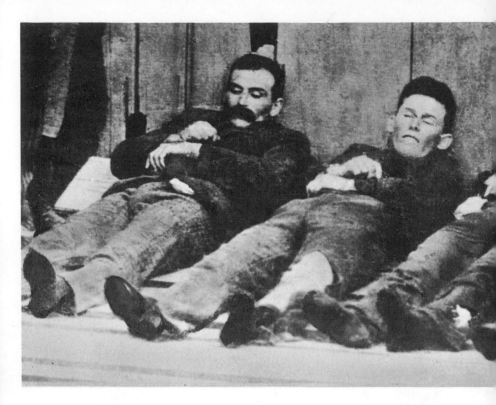

approach the prostrate forms of the dead and dying. Just as soon as their work was finished, the citizens ceased firing, shouldered their guns and gathered arund [sic] *those who had fallen in the alley. Three men lay dead in an almost direct line with each other, a fourth [Broadwell] was in the last throes of death, and a fifth was helpless and bleeding from a number of dreadful wounds. Three dead horses, smoking Winchesters, the hats of the fallen, and other evidence of a bloody conflict, were scattered over the ground where the*

134

*All were dead
but Emmet.
Left to right:
Bill Powers, Bob Dalton,
Grat Dalton,
Dick Broadwell.*

*bandits made their last stand. Grat Dalton had
kept his fake whiskers on his face, and when these
were removed the ghastly features of the man,
who had a number of acquaintances in the city
and neighborhood, were revealed. The currency
which he had secured from Condon's Bank,
amounting to nearly eleven hundred dollars, was
found on the inside of his vest, where he had evi-
dently stuffed it in a hasty manner. His Winchester, which was lying by his side, gave evidence of having been fired a number of times, but*

135

the pair of immense Colt's revolvers that were in his belt had not been discharged. Bill Powers, better known as Tom Evans, had thrown off the mask which he wore while in the bank, and his empty Winchester showed that he had taken an active part in the fight. . . . Bob Dalton had taken off his mask, and he was dead when the first man reached him. His rifle was empty, but the revolvers in his belt had not been discharged. Emmet Dalton denied his identity at first, and gave his name as Charley McLaughlin. He fell with his Winchester in his hand, the smoking muzzle of which showed that it had been very recently used. His two revolvers were in his belt, fully loaded. Each of the men had belts around their waists, containing a supply of rifle and pistol cartridges. They were all closely shaven, had on clean and comfortable clothing, and were booted and spurred in accordance with the style so prevalent in the west.

The battle was finished. All were dead but Emmet, who by some small miracle survived his twenty-three wounds. Eight people had been killed in the fight; three more were wounded. Elapsed time from the first to the last shot was but twelve minutes.

Emmet stood trial five months later. Convicted and sentenced to life imprisonment, he entered Kansas State Penitentiary in Lansing in March of 1893, soon after his twenty-first birthday. After spending fourteen-and-a-half years in prison he was pardoned. He died in Los Angeles on July 13, 1937, at the age of sixty-six.

BILL
CARLISLE
The Lone
Train Robber

LIKE BLACK BART, BILL CARLISLE WAS A LONER. BUT
he played a more dangerous game than did the famous
Po8: he went after trains full of people rather than
slow stages carrying few. There was another differ-
ence. When Carlisle was born, Black Bart, Sam Bass,
and Jesse James were already legends, and the Daltons
had not long to live; by the time Carlisle was big
enough to rob his first train, the Allies were preparing
for the German attack at Verdun.

William Carlisle was born on May 4, 1890; one of
five children. His mother died when he was nine
months old. His father placed Bill in an orphanage,
retrieving him when he was seven.

Bill was a habitual truant from school and home,
and early in his teens he left home for good. He took
to riding the rails and once helped a gang of burglars
break into a mine office for the payroll; the gang got

137

only $50 for their trouble. In 1905 he joined a circus, but soon had to flee when police attempted to arrest him for a safe-cracking in Youngstown, Ohio, a crime he did not commit. He was arrested several times as a vagrant while trying to hop freights out of Chicago. Finally, when three men tried to arrest him, he grabbed one of their guns and made them his prisoner. He handcuffed them together, took their guns and money, and went to Indianapolis where he pawned two of the guns for cash. The very next day, while he was watching a vaudeville show, he spotted a man and a girl who had been part of a swindle that had clipped him for $10. Bill waited outside until the show was over, then took more than his money back.

He turned seventeen in 1906 and decided to head west. Hopping a Chicago freight, he rode to Malta, Montana, where he got a job on a ranch. Before long a cowboy named Missouri asked him if he would take a trip to Canada with him. The "cowboy" turned out to be an ordinary horse thief.

The two riders headed for Canada driving four horses ahead of them. That afternoon they were halted by a posse and let go. They camped near the Canadian border for another day, then set the four horses free and rode back to the ranch, acting as though they had made a sale. The real purpose of the trip had been to draw the attention of the posse while others—a gang including the Skelton brothers—put a bunch of stolen horses into Canada some twenty miles away.

From then on Bill Carlisle rode often to the border with stolen stock. Missouri, meanwhile, tried to teach him how to handle a gun. Bill was accurate but slow. Missouri turned to teaching him the art of bluffing his way out of a tight spot.

One night, while camped on the Canadian side of the border, at the height of a furious electrical storm the gang was attacked by Mounties. Carlisle's horse broke the stake rope and ran off, leaving Carlisle stranded. The Skelton brothers, closely pursued by a Mountie named Keeson, suddenly came riding toward him. Bill held up his arm in the expectation of being picked up by Lou Skelton. To his surprise Lou fired at him, grazing his skull and knocking him unconscious. He came to five days later in Keeson's house.

There Carlisle learned that the gang had been broken up: Missouri had killed the Skelton brothers and fled to Denver. The others had been killed or captured. The Mountie gave Bill another chance. On his release he went to Great Falls, Montana, where he stayed for a few days before pushing on for Sheridan, Wyoming, to see a brother. As luck would have it he hitched a ride on the wrong train and ended up in Miles City, Montana, instead.

He worked there in a livery stable for a few days, then on a ranch. An accident while cutting ice resulted in a severe case of frostbite. Minor amputations of the tips of his toes and tips of some of his fingers were necessary.

Just two weeks after his feet had been operated on, he decided to leave town. He walked sixty-five miles in three days, arriving at the Smith brothers' ranch—recommended as a place where no one asked questions.

Here he remained until wanderlust came upon him and he left.

He looked up his brother, who was now working at Suddex, on the Powder River, and stayed with him for about a week. He then headed for Denver, but moved on after a poker game broke him. Texas was next, then Oklahoma, New Mexico, and Colorado again. He moved on to Wyoming, then back to Texas, where he tried his hand at running guns across the border into Mexico. Discouraged by the hazards after two trips, he took the train for Amarillo, but it was marooned by washouts during a heavy rain. Bill spotted a shipping corral near the tracks, so he checked his saddle out of the baggage car and headed for the ranch, a big one called the Matador. Here he worked as a cowboy until fall; then he was on the move again.

He wandered for the next few years, taking work when he could find it. Jobs were scarce and men were plentiful. He spent most of his time flat broke and hungry. He finally landed a job in a mine at $3.00 a day—but it operated only about three days a week. He stuck it out for a year, then quit and went to Wyoming, stopping first in Cheyenne, then Rawlins, and Rock Springs.

On February 9, 1916, Bill decided to rob a train. With five cents left in his pocket he jumped aboard the Union Pacific's Portland Rose just east of Green River, Wyoming. Armed with a glass toy gun—given by a newspaper to people who had placed want ads—and a thirty-two caliber pistol, he got $52.35 from the startled victims of the first train robbery in sixteen years.

Bill boldly went to Green River and visited a barber shop, first hiding his coat—which was identifiable as belonging to the train robber—behind a telephone pole outside. While Bill awaited his turn, a man burst into the shop with the coat. There was soon a crowd in the shop, including the town's marshal, talking about the robbery. Not suspected as the robber, Bill joined in on the conversation.

Later that night he left by train for Laramie. From there he went to Cheyenne, then on to Wheatland, and back to Cheyenne. On April 4 he hit the Overland Limited as it pulled out of Cheyenne. As he was robbing the passengers, a brakeman spotted him and notified the Cheyenne authorities but Bill escaped on foot with $506.07. He walked one hundred and fifty miles in five days, hitched an automobile ride for twenty more, and rode in a stage the last twenty miles to Douglas. He picked up another $500 in a card game before taking the train for Casper.

Carlisle was bothered by reports of others being arrested for his holdups. To clear a man jailed for the Cheyenne robbery, he dispatched a letter to the *Denver Post*, enclosing a watch chain taken from a passenger on the Overland Limited.

His letter read:

Denver Post:
To prove that this letter is the real thing, I am enclosing a watch-chain which I took from the last hold-up out of Cheyenne—this chain can easily be identified.

To convince the officers that they have the
wrong man in jail, I will hold up a train some-
where west of Laramie, Wyoming.
The White Masked Bandit

Carlisle left Casper for Greeley, Colorado, where he
booked Pullman space on the Union Pacific Limited to
Rawlins, Wyoming, west of Laramie.

Soon after the train pulled out of Hanna, Carlisle
left his seat and went to the combined observation and
smoking car. Three chorus girls and their manager
were on the rear platform. Looking around the car, Bill
realized that he could not keep the dozen or more smoking compartment passengers under his guns while
holding up the more crowded observation part of the
car. To make matters worse a guard and a brakeman
had disappeared, and he had no idea where they might
be.

The observation section made up the rear portion of
the railroad car. The smoking compartment was up forward. Carlisle walked through the smoker to the front
of the observation section where he unscrewed the
light, putting that end in darkness. He had just started
to put on his mask when the missing guard suddenly
reappeared. Bill dropped the mask, pulled his gun, and
ordered the guard to raise his hands. He marched the
guard into the smoker and ordered the passengers to
put their hands up. Leaving them there, he pushed the
guard ahead of him back into the observation section.
Next, he instructed the porter to take up the collection.
The chorus girls on the platform, meanwhile, were

quite amused by the whole affair: they watched the robbery with their faces pressed against the glass.

Bill noticed them moving their heads to see behind him. He turned to find the conductor entering the car. Firing a warning shot, Bill told the conductor to put up his hands and then boldly turned his back.

The porter finally finished collecting the passengers' money and valuables. Taking the guard, conductor, and brakeman with him, Bill moved into the smoking compartment, where the passengers still sat with their hands held high. Bill had the brakeman take up the collection. Bill went next to the Pullman car; the guard took the collection there.

Finally finished, Bill leaped from the train at what he supposed was a curve east of Walcott. He dropped into the darkness only to discover that he had left the train at the wrong spot. He missed a railroad tunnel by less than thirty feet.

With his ankle twisted, his face cut, and his body bruised from the fall, he nevertheless managed to hobble away, taking the $378.50 in loot with him, but leaving behind two guns and a billfold that belonged to the guard.

He had to remove his right shoe, and each step brought him pain. He took off his other shoe to make the walking easier. Feet bleeding from thorns and sand, and one eye swollen so that he could hardly see, he wandered all night. He hoped to reach the Medicine Bow River before daylight, but at dawn was still miles away. He washed in the Platte River; by now his right eye was nearly shut and his foot was huge.

143

Bill lay down and went to sleep, waking up a few hours later to the sound of voices. He slid into heavier brush and went back to sleep. When he awoke again it was just past three o'clock in the afternoon. A rider was searching the brush close to him. He knew that the posse was all around and that escape was hopeless. As one of the men rode past Bill's hiding spot he jumped up and covered him. A startled rider heard the outlaw say, "I've got the drop, but I'm going to give up." The rider spurred his horse and dashed away about sixty feet, jumped off his horse, and pointing his rifle at Bill, ordered him to get his hands up. Bill put his gun back in his pocket and raised his hands. The man fired anyway, but missed. Another man came riding up and the capture was complete.

Bill was tried and convicted on May 10, 1916. He was sentenced to a life term at hard labor in the State Penitentiary at Rawlins, Wyoming. In July of 1919 he applied for clemency; his sentence was reduced to fifty years. The following November Bill escaped by hiding inside a box used for shipping the shirts made in the prison's shirt factory. He made his way to Laramie, then on to Rock River, where he decided to hold up another train.

He boarded the Union Pacific, smashed the door glass of a coach and climbed in. A guard rushed forward, but Bill ordered him back. When Bill entered the main part of the coach he found the car filled with soldiers and sailors on their way home from the war in Europe; the date was November 19, 1919. Undaunted, he ordered "hands up," and made the collection himself. He robbed only half a dozen passengers, leaving the women and an old couple alone. The loot came to $86.40.

The next car was the day coach. He could see from one end of the car to the other, and he spotted a man who ducked back out of sight. Suddenly, the coach door opened and two young men, one with a gun, stood facing him. Bill knocked the man's gun up with his own, but the other's gun went off, wounding the outlaw in the hand. The two men then leaped back into the car and disappeared.

When the train came into Medicine Bow, Bill jumped off. Another man jumped from a different part of the train at the same time. Behind Bill, a man leaned out of a window and began shooting. The man who had jumped began firing also, but soon ran for cover when the bullets flying from the train threatened him as well. In the confusion Bill escaped into the hills and stayed with some friends for several days. Not wanting to endanger the people who were helping him, Bill moved on. He went, as usual, on foot. Wracked by fever from his hand wound, which by now had become infected, his progress was slow. A posse dogged his trail and got closer by the day.

His arm swelled from wrist to shoulder. He could not bend his elbow. He had been walking for two weeks, and was now so weak that he frequently stumbled and fell. The weather was bitterly cold, well below zero. He finally reached a miner's cabin, where the posse tracked him. When they arrived, Bill left his guns on the bed and stepped to the door between the bedroom and kitchen, holding his hands up. "Get them up higher," the sheriff ordered, but the swollen arm would not move. The sheriff fired, sending a rifle bullet through Bill's right lung.

Bill Carlisle was returned to prison, where he remained until his parole on January 8, 1936.

BIBLIOGRAPHY

AGEE, G. W. *Rube Burrow, King of Outlaws.* Chicago: Henneberry Company, 1890.

ADAMS, R. F. *A Fitting Death for Billy the Kid.* New York: Hastings House, 1956.

BLOCK, E. B. *Great Stagecoach Robberies of the West.* New York: Doubleday, 1962.

BREIHAN, C. W. *The Complete and Authentic Life of Jesse James.* New York: Frederick Fell, 1953.

————. *Badman of the Frontier Days.* New York: Robert M. McBride, 1957.

CARLISLE, W. L. *Bill Carlisle, Lone Bandit.* Pasadena, California: Trail's End Publishing, 1946.

CUNNINGHAM, E. *Triggernometry.* New York: Press of the Pioneers, 1934.

DALTON, E. *When the Daltons Rode.* New York: Doubleday, Doran, 1936.

The Dalton Brothers and Their Astounding Career of Crime. By an Eyewitness. New York: Frederick Fell, 1954. First published in 1892.

DOBIE, J. FRANK. *A Vaquero of the Brush Country.* Dallas, Texas: Southwest Press, 1929.

ELLIOTT, D. S. *Last Raid of the Daltons.* Coffeyville, Kansas: published by Coffeyville Daily Journal, 1892. Third edition.

147

GARD, WAYNE. *Sam Bass*. New York: Houghton Mifflin, 1936.

GARRETT, P. F. *The Authentic Life of Billy, the Kid*. Norman, Oklahoma: University of Oklahoma Press, 1954. First published in 1882.

GILLETT, J. B. *Six Years With the Texas Rangers*. New Haven: Yale University Press, 1925.

HARDIN, J. W. *John Wesley Hardin*. Norman, Oklahoma: University of Oklahoma Press, 1961. First published in 1896.

HORAN, J. D., and SWIGGERT, H. *The Pinkerton Story*. New York: G. P. Putnam, 1951.

HORAN, J. D. *Desperate Men*. New York: Doubleday, 1962.

HUNT, FRAZIER. *The Tragic Days of Billy the Kid*. New York: Hastings House, 1956.

JACKSON, J. H. *Bad Company*. New York: Harcourt, Brace, 1949.

MARTIN, C. L. *A Sketch of Sam Bass, The Bandit*. Norman, Oklahoma: University of Oklahoma Press, 1956. First published in 1880.

NORDYKE, L. *John Wesley Hardin, Texas Gunman*. New York: William Morrow, 1957.

PINKERTON, W.A. "Train Robberies." An address delivered at annual convention of International Chiefs of Police, Jamestown, Virginia, 1907.

RAINE, W. M. *Guns of the Frontier*. Boston: Houghton Mifflin, 1940.

RASCH, P. "Five Days of Battle." *Denver Westerners' Brand Book*. Volume 11, 1955.

WEBB, W. P. (ed.) *The Handbook of Texas* (two volumes). Austin, Texas: The Texas State Historical Association, 1952.

INDEX

149